Murder on the Menu

Murder on the Menu

The Sensational Story of
the Tycoon Who Founded
Saravana Bhavan

Nirupama Subramanian

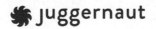

JUGGERNAUT BOOKS
C-I-128, First Floor, Sangam Vihar, Near Holi Chowk,
New Delhi 110080, India

First published by Juggernaut Books 2021

10 9 8 7 6 5 4 3 2 1

PISBN: 9789391165307
EISBN: 9789391165352

Typeset in Adobe Caslon Pro by R. Ajith Kumar, Noida

Printed at Thomson Press India Ltd

To all the front-line workers who toil bravely,
selflessly, and make it easier for the rest of us to
live through Covid-19

1

It had been an exceptionally rainy month and Kodaikanal was cooler than usual for the time of the year. As Murugesan and Raman, two guards in the Tamil Nadu government's forest department, patrolled their beat on the winding ghat road that goes from Perumal Malai to Kodai town mid-morning on 31 October 2001, there was a constant drizzle, with mist rolling in and out and the scent of wet wood hanging heavy in the air.

The two men kept their eyes on Tiger Shola, a dense grove downslope from the road. Shola (or cholai) are forest patches of native deciduous trees, shrubs and grasslands unique to the Nilgiri Hills in the southern Western Ghats. Kodaikanal, located in a spur of the Western Ghats projecting eastwards into Tamil Nadu, is at an elevation of 2133 metres. It is a hill resort-town established by the British in the nineteenth century. Its untidy expansion over the decades is the story of every 'hill station' in India. But the shola around Kodai are still magnificent, painting the slopes and the valleys in every shade of green, the trees with their thick trunks and gnarled branches, and the vines twisted over and around them testimony to the age of the forest. The Kodai sholas are even known to have tigers. Long ago, someone spotted the big cat in this stretch between Perumal Malai and Kodaikanal. That is why it is called Tiger Shola, though no one remembers when anyone last saw a tiger there. Still, there was no telling. It could always be that kind of day. In any case, so much else happens in a forest that a forest guard has to keep track of. The place was teeming with bison and elephant herds, bear and wild boar.

Every day, the two guards had to report back to the Forest Office in Kodaikanal any animal activity, usual or unusual. Or for that matter, any human activity, which in those thick woods usually meant trouble: illegal tree-felling, also tourists going close to the gaur, only to discover they are not placid buffaloes and could give chase if provoked. Raman kept an official diary in which he noted down the day's happenings.

Keeping close to the wall on the ghat road, the two guards had barely crossed the fourth mile post from Perumal Malai when Raman stopped in his tracks. Something – someone – was lying in the undergrowth some five metres below, but there wasn't a clear view from the road. He and Murugesan swung over the low parapet and, sure-footed in the way that foresters are, made their way down the wet, slippery slope.

It was a young man, and he was dead. He was lying on a patch of thick grass. New vegetation had grown around him, obstructing a clear sighting from the road. His face was bloated. The clothes suggested to Raman and his colleague that this lad had been better paid than them. Perhaps he had even been to a good school and college. In his blue checked shirt and sandal-coloured trousers he looked very much a city boy. Unidentified bodies in the jungle were not an everyday occurrence in Kodai. But there was always the possibility of a jilted lover leaping to his death, or some unfortunate tourist being attacked by a bear.

Perumal Malai today is a messy, bustling town in its own right, with homestays and guest houses for budget tourists who find Kodai too pricey. The roadsides are packed with parked cars, mini buses and small load-carriers. Crowds of youngsters go trekking up to the Perumal Malai peak, taking selfies along the way. Back in 2001, though, Perumal Malai was a small village on the Palani Ghat road to Kodai – small enough that everyone knew everyone else.

The foresters, who were also from Perumal Malai, asked local passers-by if anyone knew the man, just to rule out that he was a local. He did not look familiar. They then asked a villager to fetch Natesan, the local fireman. By the time Natesan arrived, it was 12.30 p.m. The two foresters left the fireman to guard the body and headed to the Forest Office, getting a ride in a vehicle going to Kodai. There, a senior officer told them to inform the police.

~

It was around 6.45 p.m. that the two foresters returned to the spot where the body was still being guarded by Natesan. Sub-Inspector Emmanuel Rajkumar and Head Constable Sebastian from the Kodai police station were with them. Also with them in the police jeep were two sanitation workers, Sailathnathan and John, described in police records as 'scavengers', the most polite word that officialese could come up with to refer to members of a caste group that was associated with society's 'impure' tasks. No one else would touch the body because they belonged to castes that looked down on these jobs. Though it was pitch-dark, a small crowd of local people had gathered at the spot. Head Constable Sebastian, who had brought his own camera, shot a full reel of eight frames of the body and the area where it had been found. He also made a sketch of the scene. A case under Section 174 of the Criminal Procedure Code (Cr.PC), which empowers the investigating officer to ascertain the cause of death, had already been filed at the Kodaikanal police station on the basis of Raman's complaint.

Sailathnathan and John took the body to the government hospital in Kodaikanal. Two days later, on 2 November, Dr Sivakumar at the hospital conducted the post-mortem and arrived at the following conclusions:

Time of death: approximately three to five days prior to autopsy. Death due to asphyxia on account of throttling.

Male body, aged about thirty years. Nails on both fingers and toes blue. Face, chest, abdomen, scrotum and penis slightly bloated, as the body was in the early stages of decomposition. Eyeballs and tongue bulging out. Contusion in the front and outer aspects of the right shoulder. Fracture of the greater horns of the hyoid bone, the U-shaped bone located in the neck just over the voice box that holds the tongue in place.

The post-mortem made it clear the man had been murdered. But there was a problem. The body had not been identified. It was already more than forty-eight hours since it had been found. The police had received no missing person complaint. With their small staff and resources, the Kodai police appeared to have decided it was pointless to launch a murder investigation that might linger as an unsolved crime in their precincts. But they did not close the case. From their point of view, they had carried out all the procedures correctly – taken photographs of the body and preserved the clothes and other personal effects found on the man. There was nothing more to be done. On the same day, the police had the body buried in the Hindu 'burial ground' maintained by the Kodai municipality.

But the police officers had foresight enough to know that some day someone might come looking for the body. They got the watchman at the cemetery to place a large granite stone to mark the grave. If there was to be a further police investigation and the body needed to be located, it could be found easily.

~

None of the people involved in this chain of events over those two wet days in October–November 2001 knew the importance of what they had stumbled upon. But very soon it became clear that Raman and Murugesan's discovery, and the procedures followed by the foresters, the police, the doctor and the men who buried the body, would form the main evidence in a murder investigation that spanned eight districts of Tamil Nadu and had to pass three trials at three different levels of India's judicial system over a period of nearly two decades.

The accused was Tamil Nadu's most well-known restaurateur, who ended up scripting a criminal coda to his own remarkable humble-beginnings-to-hubris story. That story may have ended differently had the body of the young man never been found, had it rolled right down the slope and plunged into the thickly wooded gorge a couple of hundred feet below, where a stream flowed fast, fed by the nearby Silver Cascades waterfall. For the killers of Prince Santhakumar, that had been the plan. But a shelf-like projection on the slope broke the fall of his body as they threw it out of their Tata Sumo. And as the body lay there, waiting to be found by forest guards Raman and Murugesan, the clock started ticking for Pitchai Rajagopal, founder of the celebrated restaurant chain Saravana Bhavan.

2

When Pitchai Rajagopal first left his home in the village of Punnaiyadi as a thirteen-year-old in 1960, all he aspired to was to work as a salesman in a grocery store in Chennai, the kind of job that many other village boys had managed to get in cities such as Coimbatore and Salem. Three decades later, Rajagopal had become a leading restaurant baron, the founder of Hotel Saravana Bhavan, the man behind Brand HSB, hailed across Tamil Nadu as the leader of a new generation of Tamil entrepreneurs in an economically emerging, post-liberalization India. By the early 1990s, the 'high-class' vegetarian fare in his restaurants, the stories of his uncompromising insistence on quality and his generosity towards his employees had become legendary, attracting clientele and jobseekers alike.

When his success story was being serialized in the Tamil magazine *Junior Post* in the late 1990s (published in 1997 as his autobiography titled *Vetrimeedu Asai Veithen* and in English as *I Set My Heart on Victory*), a reader wrote asking: 'What were your goals in your young age? Have you achieved them?'

Rajagopal, known by then as Annachi (or elder brother), replied: 'I had never thought of doing a particular business or attaining a good position in life. I only thought, even in my young age, that I should work hard, whatever work I did.'

Punnaiyadi itself was a place of modest ambitions, a village of about ninety households, almost all belonging to the Nadar agricultural caste group that had over the years transitioned to trade. It lies in the hinterland of Thoothukudi district, forty-five kilometres from the coastal town of Thoothukudi, the district capital. Leaving behind the blue waters of the placid Gulf of Mannar at Thoothukudi, the road to Punnaiyadi winds and curves past salt pans, paddy fields, little towns and villages, past scores of small wayside temples painted in multicoloured hues and an equal number of churches.

Thoothukudi is a semi-arid, drought-prone district

in the rain shadow southern zone of Tamil Nadu. Though the perennial Thamirabarani river – the only river that originates in the state, high up in the Pothigai Hills – flows through Tirunelveli and Thoothukudi before draining into the Gulf of Mannar, its water management has traditionally been poor, and people are dependent on the north-east monsoon for farming and for replenishment of their village tanks and wells. Natives of the area describe their land as *vaanam pattriya bhoomi* – land that looks towards the sky.

At the time the teenaged Rajagopal left home to find a job, agriculture had become a constant struggle in that arid region, and young men from Punnaiyadi and the villages around were leaving to find jobs in Tamil Nadu's capital Madras, as it was then called, and other cities in the state.

Toddy tapping had been the traditional occupation of the Nadar caste, but by the late nineteenth century the Nadar men had made their mark as a mercantile community with an immense capacity for hard work. Nadar traders specialized in two kinds of retail trade – stainless steel vessels, which are used in most Tamil households, and small grocery shops or provisions stores known as *malige kadai*. The community is politically influential. Kamaraj, the powerful Congress chief minister of Tamil Nadu, was a Nadar who had himself worked in a grocery shop as a teenager. Southern Tamil Nadu has produced other famous Nadars – Shiv Nadar, the industrialist and founder of HCL, was born not far from Punnaiyadi, in Tiruchendur; and the late Sivanthi Adityan, Shiv Nadar's maternal uncle, who was a media baron.

It had become the norm for Nadar men to leave the village at a young age and carve out their destiny elsewhere, and Rajagopal was no different, trying his luck at different places and in different jobs. He detailed those experiences in his autobiography, a self-promoting account of himself as a saint-entrepreneur fired by a divine call to action for a larger good. For a long time, it was distributed free at Saravana Bhavan restaurants as an inspirational rags-to-riches story.

Though Rajagopal did not grow up in poverty, the family was not well off. His father, Pitchai Nadar, had half an acre of land, but Punnaiyadi's hard-to-cultivate red soil had turned him into a wholesale trader in onions, a better way to make a livelihood than farming. Mostly, it was Rajagopal's mother, Mani Ammal, who tended to the small parcel of family land and the few cattle that they reared. Rajagopal says he would help her plant palmyra and help his father water the land. But even as a ten-year-old he understood that there was no money in it.

The first time he left home was when he was just out of class 5. He ran away to Madras, as Chennai was known until 1996, hoping to work in a paternal uncle's grocery shop in Mylapore. But the reception he received there was far from warm – the disapproving uncle wrote to inform his parents that their son had fetched up there. Rajagopal, who had stolen money from his father's pouch before running away to Madras, decided that the better part of valour was to go back home. He left without telling the uncle and returned to Punnaiyadi as quietly as he had departed. Two years later, after he had passed his class 7 exams, his parents gave in to his insistence that he be allowed to go and work in a grocery shop in Coimbatore. On day one, he found himself appointed as the cook for all the others who worked there. Years later, feeding others would become his life's business. But at this point he was clueless in the kitchen. He feigned illness and was sent home on the third day.

Despite the repeated setbacks, he was determined

to get out of Punnaiyadi. 'My friends were the reason for this. Many of them had studied only up to class 5, and they had jobs. When they came back to the village during their holidays, they would wear stylish, colourful clothes. They would have money and spend lavishly. I too longed for the time when I would have a job, earn and spend according to my will and pleasure,' he wrote in *I Set My Heart on Victory*.

His third foray out of the village was to Valparai in the Annamalai Hills, where he found a job as a cleaner at a small eatery called D'Navis, owned by a man who was also from Punnaiyadi. The proprietor would hand over Rajagopal's monthly salary of Rs 25 to his parents during his monthly visits to Punnaiyadi. Rajagopal took to his job with gusto. 'As I wanted to be appreciated by the elders for my hard work and earnestness, I was never slack in what I did. I was particular in getting appreciation for my work as a cleaner,' he recalled in the memoir. The proprietor treated him kindly, but then Rajagopal fell ill with a fever and had to go back to Punnaiyadi to recover. He did not return to Valparai. His fourth attempt out of Punnaiyadi led him to a grocery store in Coimbatore, but that ended badly when the shop owner beat him over a mistake. The fifth time he left Punnaiyadi he was fifteen, and it was back to his uncle's shop in Madras, and from then on there was no looking back.

~

Almost equidistant from Punnaiyadi are two big towns, Thoothukudi and Tirunelveli, on the northern bank of the Thamirabarani river. For the religious tourism trail, the entire belt is a gold mine. The most common type of traveller in this region is the pilgrim. Large buses ferry pilgrims back and forth on the state highways. Of the eighteen temples of note in the area, the nine dedicated to Shiva are known in pilgrim lore as Nava Kailasam, and the nine dedicated to Vishnu as Nava Tirupati. But the circuit is not just restricted to Hindu temples.

Churches affiliated to various Christian denominations – Roman Catholic, Seventh Day Adventist, Church of South India, Lutheran, Assembly of God – neighbour the temples, and do their bit for the pilgrim economy too. Christianity came to Tuticorin (as Thoothukudi was called in colonial times) in the sixteenth century with the Portuguese, and every subsequent conqueror, drawn to the place by its natural harbour, the pearls in the water and the cotton trade, brought in their own brand of the religion. The Dutch built the first Protestant church here in 1750.

To this mix of temples and churches, Pitchai Rajagopal added his own grand new religious edifice in 2009.

Rajagopal had grown up in a devoutly religious family. A large bell at the temple in his mother's village had his father's name inscribed on it – his father had donated the bell to the temple, his mother told him, when a persistent and painful sore on his back had been cured by divine intervention after he prayed there. In Punnaiyadi, his parents, like other Hindu villagers, would bow facing east twice a day, once in the morning and then in the evening. Rajagopal picked up the habit in childhood without knowing why, but realized as he grew up that to the east was Tiruchendur, famous for its temple dedicated to the peacock-riding boy-god Muruga – the second son of Shiva and Parvathi, brother of Ganesha – who also goes by the name Saravana.

In Tamil Nadu, as elsewhere, the quickest way for successful businessmen to cement their position in society is by becoming patrons of religion and culture. As we shall see later, by 2009 Rajagopal was in trouble with the law and his image as a do-gooding hotelier had begun to unravel. He desperately wanted to recover the esteem and respect he had lost after the shocking disclosure of his role as the mastermind of the murder of a young man. A young man whose wife he was pursuing, despite being married to two other women at the same time. In 2004, a trial court had convicted him of the lesser offence of culpable homicide not amounting to murder. As he appealed the sentence in the Madras High Court, Rajagopal poured Rs 5 crore into building the Vana Tirupati temple in Punnaiyadi. It had shiny brown and beige granite floors and tall columns, and its walls were adorned with murals of the ten avatars of Vishnu on one side and with godly scenes painted in calendar-art style on the other. The temple's main idol of Vishnu as Sri Sreenivasa Perumal is a replica of the one at Tirupati in Andhra Pradesh.

By the time Vana Tirupati was inaugurated in late 2009, the Madras High Court had rejected Rajagopal's appeal and handed down a tougher punishment – a life sentence for murder. But Rajagopal appealed the verdict in the Supreme Court and received a stay on imprisonment pending the court's decision. He then went ahead and organized a grand kumbabhishekam, or consecration of the temple, complete with music recitals by a number of artistes, among them the well-known Carnatic vocalist Nityashree Jayaraman.

Did Rajagopal hope his lavish act of piety would ensure divine intervention to save him from the clutches of the law? D. Vasanthan, an employee of Saravana Bhavan since 1991, who was hand-picked by Rajagopal as the 'senior manager' of the temple, has a different theory about why his boss built the temple. According to him, Rajagopal, whom he regards as next only to God, built the temple to counter the spread of Christianity in the region. 'You would have seen the number of churches that have come up in this area. If you take this village itself, 40 per cent people are Christian. He wanted to stop Hindus from converting to Christianity. Now Hindus in this area have something to be proud of,' said Vasanthan, and added, 'After the temple came up, there have been fewer conversions.' Vasanthan's theory is certainly one that will gladden the hearts of those who want Hindutva to take root in Tamil Nadu, where religious communalism has so far found little space. But it also seems evident that Rajagopal believed that observing superstitions, looking for omens, constantly supplicating the deities and obsessively performing religious rituals would bring him everything he wanted – wealth, respect, the woman he lusted after and, of course, most important of all, acquittal by the Supreme Court.

But whatever Rajagopal's motivation, it is undeniable that the grand Vana Tirupati temple he built has ensured that the village where he was born and grew up became more than a mere dot on the map, its name now upgraded to Punnai Nagar. There was a time when state transport buses would skip Punnaiyadi, it used to be that small and desolate a hamlet. It did not even qualify to be called a village. In Tamil, such places are known as kugramam. Residents recall that when the bus stopped at the next village of Neivilai, people who had wanted to get down at Punnaiyadi would hasten as they walked back after getting off the bus, afraid they would be attacked by wayside robbers lurking in the bordering patch of scrub forest. But today, big white tourist buses disgorge streams of pilgrims and other passengers at a well-lit purpose-built parking bay next to the Vana Tirupati temple, now the biggest and most significant temple in the panchayat of seventeen villages, of which Punnaiyadi is a part.

The ninety houses in the village are built along a

single paved lane. The temple is at the top of this lane. While the god Ganesha gets pride of place at the entrance to the temple, to one side are two life-sized sculptures of a couple seated next to each other, both painted in a golden shade. The couple are Rajagopal's late parents, Pitchai Nadar and Mani Ammal. Inside, a voice recording in Tamil plays on loop, narrating the history of the temple. Rajagopal's name comes up repeatedly. Photographs of the kumbabhishekam hang on the walls, and Rajagopal and his wife are prominent in the photographs mounted on a specially erected board in the forecourt of the temple. Three shops in the forecourt sell temple bric-a-brac, temple laddoos and religious books. Temporary shops outside sell toys, caps and other kitsch, an opportunity for people from the villages around to earn a living.

Inside, pilgrims file past the main Vishnu deity, drink fragrant tulsi water that the priest spoons out of a steel jug into their cupped palms, and circumambulate the temple, stopping at every shrine around the main sanctum sanctorum before finally prostrating themselves outside the sanctum. A priest was flown down from Tirupati to train eight local Brahmin priests from the nearby village of Alwarthirunagar, Vasanthan said.

As devotees move on towards the exit, a man hands them prasadam on a small piece of a banana leaf. It has been made by Brahmin cooks, who also received training in Tirupati. They learned, among other things, to make laddoos exactly the way they are made at Tirupati. Tamil Nadu's Perumal kovils (temples dedicated to Vishnu) have far more interesting offerings than the Shivan kovils. At Perumal temples the prasadam is usually curd rice, tamarind rice, pongal, or rava kesri – bright yellow suji halwa dripping with ghee, studded with plump raisins and cashews. Rajagopal's temple in remote Punnaiyadi is no different in this respect from other Perumal kovils, but here the well-mixed thayir saadam – the rice soft and still warm, the curd milky, perfectly seasoned with tiny, precisely cut bits of ginger and green chilli – only seems to underline the temple's gastronomical connections. Hotel Saravana Bhavan's curd rice was at one time among its biggest hits.

Of course, the only restaurant in one-lane Punnaiyadi is – what else – a Saravana Bhavan, right opposite the temple. Visiting pilgrims flock to the restaurant, but the local people don't eat there. Indeed, few people remain in Punnaiyadi, most of them having left to work in cities elsewhere in Tamil Nadu. Only seven or eight men and about fourteen women and a few children now live in the village, according to Vasanthan. The restaurant and the temple, both managed by Saravana Bhavan, together employ some 130 people, five times its resident adult population. They are mostly from villages around Punnaiyadi, while some are on transfer from other Saravana Bhavan branches. Staffers who do not have homes nearby live in a dormitory built for them.

Besides building the temple, Rajagopal also bought up 50 acres of land from the village residents. Vasanthan said it was wasteland that had almost been abandoned by the owners. Rajagopal turned most of this around as farmland, with locals employed to cultivate it. It was on a portion of this land that the restaurant came up, with another part levelled for the parking area.

The houses in Punnaiyadi remain old-style 'street houses' with a thinnai, or front veranda, flush with the lane. The biggest house is different. It is a boxy Agra sandstone–coloured structure with two wings, and a lot of dark tinted glass and steel thrown in. It's the only one with three gates – one for the parking area, another for the main entrance to the house, and a third, smaller gate. Rajagopal built this house in 1994 over the modest old family home, at a time when Saravana Bhavan was on an unstoppable expansion spree across Chennai. He named it Mani Ammal Illam, after his mother, and had the name inscribed on a small slab of maroon granite embedded in one of the gateposts. A similar slab of granite on another gatepost has the names of Rajagopal and Valli Ammal, his wife.

Valli Ammal's name is emblazoned across a building next door too, between the house and the restaurant. It houses Hotel Chendur Murugan, which is also run by Saravana Bhavan. It looks empty, but Vasanthan said when people of the village who work outside return for occasions like a marriage or a funeral, they take rooms in the hotel rather than spend their time cleaning their locked-up houses to make them habitable again.

The Saravana Bhavan complex – temple, restaurant, hotel and shops – is now bigger than the village. The pilgrims don't seem to know or care about the notoriety now attached to Rajagopal's name, and if they have heard of him, they are surprised to learn of his association with this village. For the few people left in Punnaiyadi, and for the Saravana Bhavan employees, Rajagopal is still the much-admired son of the soil who broke through to the premier league of the world outside but did not forget his roots. No one talks about 'the case'.

It is an off-limits topic for the people of Punnaiyadi.

Arumugham Balachandran, who lives a few doors down the lane from Rajagopal's house, says whatever 'development' came to the village, it was thanks to Rajagopal, whom he called his friend of many years. 'He did a lot for this small ooru [hamlet]. Everything you see here is thanks to him.'

'There are other famous and more successful Nadar in this area,' says Vasanthan. 'They may give money to their village temples or for other causes. But they do not get involved themselves. They fly in and they fly out. Rajagopal was one of those rare persons who remained rooted in Punnaiyadi.' Despite his hectic schedule running his restaurant empire, Rajagopal would visit Punnaiyadi every alternate week, driving into the village in his Mercedes on a Friday, staying at his home and leaving on Sunday.

~

In his mind's eye, he may have envisioned Punnaiyadi emerging as an important temple town in its own corner of Tamil Nadu. It may have been his dream that Punnaiyadi under his patronage would one day host its own music and dance festivals, at which celebrity classical vocalists and dancers would perform. Audiences would flock in from far and wide, imparting their energy to the village. They would stay in the hotel, and their morning coffee and breakfast would be sent up to their rooms from the Saravana Bhavan next door. And through the day there would be music ringing through the temple . . .

He may have convinced himself he would emerge from this 'nuisance' of a murder case, acquitted by the Supreme Court.

After all, since he left this desolate little hamlet as a teenager, hadn't he proved himself capable of overcoming every obstacle to find fame and fortune in the big wide world?

3

When he arrived in Madras as a fifteen-year-old, Rajagopal worked for a few days in his paternal uncle's grocery store in Mylapore, then moved to a job in a Nadar steel utensils shop, in which he stayed for five or six years until he became restless to do his own thing. He started his own provisions store in a run-down part of Kodambakkam, moving in 1972 to Ashok Nagar, then an up-and-coming middle-class neighbourhood. Despite some ups and downs, his provisions business grew, and soon he had three stores, including one in KK Nagar, a neighbourhood close to Ashok Nagar. He called all his shops Murugan Stores. The motto of the shops was 'Quality, High Quality'.

'We would never pass off to the customers an inferior

product as superior. We would quote the correct price ... we quote the same price [for a particular item] ... whether the customer was a boy or a bigwig,' Rajagopal would say in his memoir.

KK Nagar was at the time considered the boonies of Chennai, still to become the congested middle-class maze of flats it is today. Salesmen who came to unload goods at Rajagopal's provisions store there complained there was nowhere to grab a proper bite in the area. They would want to get done with the unloading and the payments quickly so that they could go to T Nagar, 5 kilometres away, where there were plenty of eating places serving modestly priced but filling rice meals. A plan began to take shape in Rajagopal's entrepreneurial head: not only did this area need a restaurant, the city needed a new kind of eatery where middle-class families could come for a tasty, modestly priced meal, served in clean and pleasant surroundings.

~

In the 1970s and 1980s, in the years before the dramatic opening up of India's economy, when Chennai was still staid Madras, eating out was not the popular pastime it would become in the 1990s. Family dining-out those days was largely restricted to the affluent or to well-paid professionals. And there was only a handful of restaurants that catered to such a clientele, if one didn't count the five-star hotels and the members-only dining rooms of elite clubs.

People's tastes had not yet expanded to accommodate the flavours of the world. *The Hindu*'s first food writer and her adventures in Italian restaurants were two decades away, as were the Thai, Mexican and Korean restaurants and French bakeries that now dot Chennai. The city's only Chinese restaurant was in the five-star Taj Hotel, until in the mid-1980s a well-appointed restaurant called Cascades opened, giving Madras its first taste of authentic 'Indian-Chinese', with a menu that was kind enough to include vegetarian noodles and spicy aubergine in garlic sauce along with non-vegetarian fare such as beef oriental pepper fry and crispy lamb honey chilli. In a meeting of destinies, the man who started Cascades, M. Mahadevan, would partner with Saravana Bhavan a quarter of a century later. A 'baked dish' made its first appearance outside club and five-star portals perhaps for the first time in the late 1980s, at a small restaurant called Eden. In the 1970s, the opening of a restaurant in Mylapore serving chhole bhature was enough to send a frisson of excitement through the conservative Brahmin community that lived in the area.

Contrary to popular perception, over 90 per cent of Tamil Nadu is meat-eating, with vegetarianism largely confined to the Brahmins. All the same, vegetarianism is also widely regarded as next only to godliness, and at one time it was unthinkable to eat meat outside the privacy of the home. Even today, meat shops are euphemistically called 'protein shops', which was why, in those pre-liberalization years, Chennai's 'military hotels', with their 'protein'-heavy menu, were the city's best-kept open secret (the limousines of Tamil film stars would often be seen outside these hole-in-the-wall places, loading massive tiffin carriers with the non-veg fare to eat in their homes, studios or sets). City historians say military hotels came up to cater to soldiers, as if there was a societal consensus that those who guard our frontiers be allowed to eat non-vegetarian fare in public. By the 1950s, they were being frequented by anyone craving non-vegetarian fare. Only men ever walked into these rough-and-ready places churning out hot and spicy 'pepper fry' meat and chicken carrying a Chettinad signature.

In those days, the stand-out 'family' non-vegetarian restaurant was Buharis, famous for its biryani, parotta and Chicken 65, which they claim to have invented, its tables laid with made in England crockery. Back then, the now-ubiquitous air-conditioned Chettinad fine-dining establishments with Carnatic muzak wafting through them, and such non-veg delights as crab varuval and mutton kozhambu on elaborately printed menu cards had yet to appear on the Madras food scene.

Of course, Madras had a plethora of small, strictly vegetarian idli–dosa cafes, but these were also frequented only by men. From the 1950s, a lot of young men began pouring into Madras from other parts of Tamil Nadu looking for work, and these were the modest eateries that fed them. You didn't see families eating there, and they were not places where a group of women could go either, even for coffee.

There was an even simpler no-frills type of place called 'mess' that came up at that time, and these too were frequented only by men. Some of these were meant only for clientele of a particular caste and were not shy of declaring that in their names, as in Brahmin Mess or Chettiar Mess. Entry was not officially barred to others, but people tended to stick to their own caste mess because inter-dining was still uncommon. Two of these are still going strong in the city, but as secular restaurants: Rayar's Mess and Karpagambal Mess, Brahmins-only when they began, both situated in still-conservative Mylapore. Diners here are encouraged to vacate their place at multi-seater tables as soon as they finish. The constant coming and going of waiters with buckets of sambar and chutneys, the clatter of steel utensils, and orders for dosais and adais being screamed into a dark kitchen at the far end are all part of 'mess' experience even now. The fare at Rayar's has not changed over the years: idli–vadai–pongal with piping hot sambar and chutney in the morning, and in the evening – it's open only until 7 p.m. – just dosas.

The enduring appeal of idli–dosa restaurants, popular even with avowed non-vegetarians, is that they are businesslike, anytime eateries, and apart from a 'full meal' comprising three courses of rice at lunchtime, they efficiently roll out a smorgasbord of snacks at any time of night or day. A serving of two fluffy idlis with a creamy coconut chutney and sambar made just right hits the spot at breakfast, at lunch, for elevenses or as a teatime snack. But in pre-liberalization Madras, if a family wanted to go out to eat a well-made pure-veg meal, in clean and pleasant surroundings, there wasn't much choice – it was either Dasaprakash or Woodlands.

The old elite of Chennai still speak with nostalgia about Dasaprakash, a traditional Udipi restaurant. There was a touch of Mysore glamour about it. It was the kind of place you dressed up to go to eat a golden-brown Mysore masala dosa and its house ice cream served in nice glass bowls. But the place went into decline by the 1980s, and in the new millennium, its building, with its distinctive art deco facade, was torn down to make way for a modern residential high-rise.

Similar to Dasaprakash was Woodlands – not quite as stylish but also a 'high-class' Udipi chain of restaurants where families could dine together. The jewel in the crown of this chain was Woodlands Drive-In, generally known as Woodies, and abbreviated to WDI, set in eighteen acres of wooded land at the end of Cathedral Road where it met Gemini Circle. Over the decades it had established itself as the go-to place for the young and old, lovers, lawyers, rich film stars in their showy long Impalas, and middle-class families in their Premier Padminis. Its parking lot with massive rain trees, their leafy branches spread out like a giant green umbrella constantly shedding feathery pink-white flowers, was the main restaurant, though it also had seating indoors. The clientele were all regulars who spent hours in the place, sometimes ordering nothing but a coffee. The waiters had been around from the time the restaurant began in 1962, and knew everyone.

It was taken over by the government after the restaurant's lease expired a few years ago and converted into a botanical garden, but in the closing decade of the twentieth century, Woodies still exuded a 1960s charm in its forest-like seclusion on one side of the city's busiest traffic junction named after the famous Gemini Studios that used to be located across the road. The studio later moved from here, and in its place came The Park, a five-star hotel.

If you visited WDI in your car, you would drive into the parking lot and grab the first empty slot. A waiter would clip an aluminium tray to the rolled-down window of your Premier Padmini or Ambassador. He would set down a glass of water on it and take your order. And you sat in the comfort of your non-AC car, on rexine-covered seats, and ate your ghee roast masala dosa, or bhakala bhaath, while the waiter checked in now and then to find out if you wanted anything more.

It was in this rather limited culinary landscape that Hotel Saravana Bhavan made a quiet entry in 1981.

~

By 1976, with his three provisions stores up and running, Rajagopal had put up a two-storeyed building in KK Nagar, naming it Tiruchendur Murugan Illam, with a loan from the Tamil Nadu Mercantile Bank. He writes in his memoir that his friend K. Ramanujam, on whose property in KK Nagar he had set up his third provisions store, pledged his property for the bank loan. Later, Ramanujam would be one of his two partners in Saravana Bhavan. As the building was being constructed, Rajagopal ran short of money to complete it. He sold his wife's jewellery, but was still short. Rajagopal was about to give up. Again, it was Ramanujam who advised him not to throw in the towel. Ramanujam then bailed out Rajagopal by lending him twenty sovereigns of gold (160 grams), with which he raised another loan from the bank to finish the construction.

The idea was to rent out part of the building as shops. And though Rajagopal wanted to start a restaurant himself on the first floor, he decided to lease it out to someone who had more experience than him in the food business. He also moved his KK Nagar Murugan Stores into the building. But the rentals from the shops and the restaurant proved inadequate to repay the loans, and the provisions store began to suffer as there was not enough money to keep it stocked.

Selling the building was the only option. Rajagopal's memoir says that Rathna Nadar, a well-known transport company owner from Thoothukudi, the same part of Tamil Nadu as Rajagopal came from, and a man from the same caste as he, made an offer. He also allowed Rajagopal to run his provisions store out of the building as a tenant. Murugan Stores was back in business. But opening his own restaurant was still a worm in Rajagopal's head, and he began eyeing Kamatchi Bhavan, the 'hotel' (as many restaurants in Tamil Nadu are called) on the first floor of the building. It was making losses, and the owner was persuaded to sell at a price that Rajagopal could afford.

Rajagopal roped in Ramanujam and, he recounts in his memoir, another friend in the area – Ganapathy Iyer, a customs official – as his partners. 'Take leave of absence from your job for five years. If the hotel business succeeds, you can resign, otherwise you go back to your job, and I will return to the village,' Rajagopal told him. He confided in Rathna Nadar that he was also encouraged by indications in his horoscope that he would 'prosper in the food business'.

Before anything else, the restaurant had to be renamed. For Rajagopal, the new name was a no-brainer. His provision shops were all named Murugan Stores. The building was called Murugan Illam, or the home of Murugan. Like most devout Hindus in Tamil Nadu, Rajagopal was an ardent devotee of Murugan and a regular visitor to the Murugan temple in the nearby town of Thiruthani. Saravana is another name for Murugan. It was a natural choice as the name for the restaurant. Saravana Bhavan opened its doors on 14 December 1981 in a run-down corner on the outskirts of what was then Madras.

4

'Eat 23 items for Rs 5'. That was the surprise that Rajagopal sprang on KK Nagar on the first anniversary of the opening of the first Saravana Bhavan. It turned out to be an immensely satisfying day for Rajagopal, a newbie seeking to make a mark in Chennai's crowded idli–dosa–meals-ready 'hotel' scene. He had done no special advertising – the restaurant had simply started selling the 5-rupee tokens for the 'special' meal to its customers from a week before. On the anniversary, the restaurant opened its doors at 10 a.m. and continued to sell its special meals as well as items from its regular menu, without a break, until 10 p.m. Business was brisk. At one point the police had to be called in to regulate the crowds. The buzz Saravana Bhavan managed to create with this gimmick resonated beyond KK Nagar, and other established restaurants in the same category – vegetarian, South Indian, open-all-day – woke up to the new kid on the block.

By the time of the second anniversary, in 1983, Rajagopal had moved to the most prized location in the city – the same T Nagar that suppliers to his grocery stores headed to for lunch after dropping off goods at his shop. With its sari and jewellery stores, T Nagar was always packed with shoppers. If they were not buying for weddings, they were buying for some other occasion – a housewarming, a birth, a birthday. Even Tuesdays, considered inauspicious for new beginnings, were crowded at T Nagar. And eating places were a mandatory pit stop during these shopping safaris. Leasing a place there was going to be expensive. But his confidence boosted by the success at KK Nagar, Rajagopal decided to go for broke. He found a vacant property in crowded Usman Road and introduced something that was not available at the time in other restaurants of that category – he fitted it with an AC room. He toured restaurants in Bengaluru to study AC rooms in restaurants there to get it right, just the way he would study Nirula's in Delhi many years later to get his own brand of ice cream right. Those who opted to sit and enjoy their coffee and Mysore bondas in AC comfort would have to pay more. And, sure enough, they did. In 1983, Rajagopal bought his first car, a second-hand Ambassador.

After this, the 1980s went by in a blur of new branches of Saravana Bhavan, one after the other – Ashok Nagar, Pursawalkam, George Town, Peter's Road, just off Mount Road (now Anna Salai), close to the most prized commercial real estate in Chennai.

But it was the Saravana Bhavan outlet opened in 1994 at Radhakrishnan Salai, sandwiched between a posh marriage hall run by the AVM family (of the film studios fame) and Nilgiris, Chennai's first supermarket, that was Rajagopal's breakout move in the city.

RK Salai – the erstwhile Edward Elliots Road – was renamed after the former president S. Radhakrishnan, whose family home still stands there. The road leads straight to the iconic Gandhi statue standing sentinel at Marina Beach, where it forms a T-junction with Beach Road. In the 1990s, RK Salai was known as the 'VIP road'. It ran the length of the northern boundary of Mylapore. Woodlands was at the western end of this boundary. Nestling within was old Mylapore, with its temples and mada streets (streets surrounding temples), music sabhas and Brahmins with their conservative eating habits, and traditional eateries like Rayar's and Karpagambal.

Chief ministerial motorcades – whether it was Jayalalithaa's from her home in Poes Garden, or M. Karunanidhi's from his home in Gopalapuram – took that road to the Secretariat at St George's Fort, past the beach and the Indo-Saracenic style Madras University and Napier's Bridge over the stinky Cooum river. At the T-junction of RK Salai and Beach Road stood the grand headquarters of the Tamil Nadu Police, an expansive beach-facing structure built in 1839 as a Masonic Lodge. At the centre of the T-junction's little roundabout is a miniature tower clock, painted an almost Wedgewood blue with roman numerals in gold. It chimes the hours, and is maintained by Simpsons, a British-era engineering firm. Everything about RK Salai screamed elite, establishment and tradition, conservative and colonial heritage, and, of course, high visibility.

When Rajagopal burst into this little bubble with his Saravana Bhavan, all clean and shiny steel, it made just the impact that he wanted. Morning walkers did the routine 3 kilometres on the Beach Road promenade from the Gandhi statue to the Labour Statue, doubled back to their starting point, got into their cars or hopped on to their scooters, or continued on foot, heading to the Saravana Bhavan on RK Salai (it became popularly known as AVM Saravana Bhavan) for their morning coffee, if not the full nine yards of idli–vada–pongal with sambar and chutney. Rajagopal too stopped by most mornings after his walk on the beach, accompanied by trusted managers.

He would start checking on every restaurant personally each morning from about four-thirty, asking about staff attendance, breakfast footfalls, inventory and kitchen status, mostly over the phone. At the AVM Saravana Bhavan, he would sit in his car and taste the coffee, sambar and chutney, doing the same at three or four of his other restaurants along the way back home.

Old faithfuls would still swear by the idli–vada–coffee at Woodlands, just a few metres away, but Saravana Bhavan had by then seeped into Chennai's culinary map and changed its eating habits before anyone realized it.

~

What made Saravana tick? After all, Rajagopal was not offering any exotic new dish that was not available at any of the other eateries in the city. He was, however, determined that his 'hotels' would be different. Even if it was the same old fare that everyone ate at home, and at other restaurants, Rajagopal wanted it to be different enough to hold people's attention and make them return again and again. His friend and business associate Mahadevan, Chennai's foremost restaurateur whose Hot Breads bakery chain made bread fashionable in Madras at a time when it was dismissed as the food of the sick, recounts the many ways in which he ensured that once you ate at Saravana Bhavan you kept coming back.

'He would say, "I don't want a person to come to my restaurant to eat because he is hungry, I want a person who comes here for the taste,"' recalls Mahadevan. Hunger is pasi and taste is rusi in Tamil, and Rajagopal was apparently quite pleased with his rhyming one-liner.

Rajagopal loved his food. He particularly loved spicy non-vegetarian fare from the deep south, his favourite karimeen fish dishes prepared by his wife Valli Ammal in her kitchen, with the spices freshly ground on her old grinding stone. Left to himself Rajagopal might have decided that Saravana Bhavan would cater to non-vegetarians too. But, as it turned out, it would be a vegetarian-only restaurant – that was the condition on which Ganapathy Iyer, the customs official who became his business partner, and who was a Brahmin and a vegetarian, had offered his support.

'But Rajagopal also saw it as a good business decision. He would say everyone eats vegetarian but not everyone eats non-vegetarian. He was seeing a bigger canvas with vegetarian food,' says Mahadevan. 'All the people in the food industry here respect him for what he has done for vegetarian food. For a person who was not a Brahmin to start a vegetarian restaurant, get Brahmins to come and eat there, and make a success of it, that's a huge thing.'

One way in which he achieved this was by getting banana leaves cut to fit and line the steel thalis in his restaurant. Now a common practice in south Indian restaurants, this was a Saravana Bhavan innovation, introduced so that people would get over their reluctance to eat off plates on which others before them had eaten. It also made the thalis easier to clean.

'He gave idli–dosa a status that it did not have before,' says Mahadevan, who introduced Chennai not only to Chinese food with Cascades and bread rolls and soup sticks but also to Thai and Mexican cuisine, delicate French pastries and other international culinary adventures that would have been unthinkable just thirty years earlier.

Mahadevan was once described by *The Hindu* as a 'serial restaurateur', and when I met him at the end of 2019, it was at one of his latest ventures – a coffee shop in a new chain called Writer's Cafe, which he described as a philanthropic venture. It was an all-women crew at the baking station, and he pointed out with pride that they were all acid attack survivors.

~

'High class' is how Rajagopal described his food to differentiate it from the meals-ready places that were a dime a dozen across Madras then. And what, according to him, went into making it high class was its 'high-quality' ingredients, sourced from the right places.

There was no cutting corners at Saravana Bhavan – the vegetables had to be fresh, the idlis made with the best urad dal and idli rice so they would turn out fluffy and soft and white, like a jasmine flower. The dosais were roasted in ghee to the correct shade of golden, and the sambar had to have just the right consistency and seasoning. And there could be no compromises on the standards he had fixed – everything had to taste exactly the same at every Saravana outlet, from the sambar to the chutney to the potato filling in the dosa, and the taste and temperature of the coffee.

'In our Saravana Bhavan hotels, a dosa weighs exactly 60 grams, the stipulated weight. It may weigh 5 grams more, but will not weigh even a gram less,' was Rajagopal's boast.

A senior employee who has been with Saravana Bhavan since the 1990s recalled how the red chillies for the house sambar powder would come from wholesalers in Guntur, and the tamarind from Tumkur in Karnataka – 'because that is where we got the type of tamarind with the right balance of sweet and tangy'. And for the same reason, the tomatoes would come from Hassan, also in Karnataka. The coffee makers learnt to mix the brew from experts at the Coimbatore-based Annapoorna chain.

Each Saravana Bhavan had its own kitchen and chef, yet the taste of the sambar at each of the outlets was identical. Many of Rajagopal's rivals hold that to be one of the biggest achievements of the chain. Stories are legion about how Rajagopal would sample the sambar from every unit to make sure that it tasted exactly the same. Mostly the samples would be delivered at his place in the morning, but he would also drop in at outlets like the one on RK Salai to do the tasting on-site.

'The colour, consistency and taste will be the same at all Saravana units,' said Mahadevan. 'That was the perfection of the training, the repeated making of the same thing. He made sure that the guy making the coffee never made sambar, the guy making the chutney did not make the sambar. It was that kind of specialization,' said Mahadevan.

In his autobiography, Rajagopal proudly wrote that his determination to uphold standards and the meticulousness with which the food was prepared scripted his success: 'Success was not easily achieved … It was due to the hard work put in by me and partner Ganapathy without even a 10-minute rest in a day,' he said about his first outlet. 'We used to be in the kitchen day and night. Discussing with the concerned specialists the kinds of ingredients that could be used for various foodstuffs. We experimented, we improved the taste of each and every item in our hotel. We supplied our cook nothing but the best vegetables.'

Complaints about the food were taken seriously. Once, a photographer who went to Malaysia on a wedding shoot bought a packet of Saravana's savoury mix – basically comprising sev mixed with peanuts and other crispies – at the Saravana Bhavan outlet in Kuala Lumpur, and found so much red chilli powder in it that his hands turned red. Months later, he ran into Rajagopal walking on Marina Beach. 'I went up and complained about it. In front of me, he called the Malaysia outlet and fired the guy who was in charge of making that mix,' the photographer recalled.

The icing on the cake, or more appropriately, the tempering in the sambar, was the emphasis on cleanliness.

'He made the restaurant so nice and clean, with waiters in neat uniforms and a dash of vibhuti [holy ash] on the forehead,' says Mahadevan, 'that going to Saravana Bhavan became an outing' – rather than just a place for a quick meal.

All staffers, and not just waiters, wore uniforms. Hygiene was a top priority, and it began with the employees' personal cleanliness. Rajagopal even paid for employees' haircuts and provided them with a toiletries kit that included nail clippers and soap. Rajagopal would say that his early stint as a cleaner in D'Navis at Valparai had taught him the importance of keeping things spick-and-span. The proprietor of D'Navis was particular about cleanliness, Rajagopal would recall. 'He would ask us to clean the dining tables . . . He would tell us to wear well-washed clothes . . . He would always be in clothes spotlessly white like the lotus flower. One wearing dirty clothes would feel shy of standing by his side.'

As he expanded and made Saravana Bhavan a chain, Rajagopal also added new items to the menu, introducing unusual dishes such as 'kaima idli', which was idli chopped up and deep fried, and served covered with a masala of onions, tomatoes and chillies. It was the colour of tandoori chicken, the idli bits looked like chunks of meat, and it was specially appealing to those who missed an 'NV' item on the Saravana menu. Kaima idli was all the rage in the 1990s. It became synonymous with the restaurant. Google the dish, and you will find several recipes put up by enterprising men and women for 'Saravana's Kaima Idli', 'like what I ate at Saravana Bhavan many years ago'.

His other hit was the adai–aviyal combo. Adai is a thick dosai or pancake, but made with several types of lentils ground together; unlike dosai, it does not contain any rice. Aviyal is a stew made out of coconut, green chillies and cumin ground together, and cooked with a mix of boiled vegetables and curd. Both are common dishes in Tamil homes, but usually eaten separately. He made the combination click.

~

In the years that followed the opening of the first Saravana Bhavan, Rajagopal and his restaurant would get written about in newspapers and magazines, not just for the quality of the food but for the amazingly generous and benevolent way they treated their employees. In Chennai's restaurant scene, if you were a waiter at a Saravana Bhavan, you had arrived in job heaven.

Right from the start, Rajagopal was clear on both these fronts – quality of ingredients and welfare of his staff. He was appalled when the experienced restaurant manager who helped him set up the first HSB outlet advised keeping costs down by buying discarded, leftover vegetables from wholesale markets and choosing lower-quality ingredients. The manager told Rajagopal he shouldn't pay the staff more than Rs 3–4 per day – since they were usually people who had run away from their homes, 'this wage is enough'. Though Rajagopal was quite dependent on this manager to guide him through the setting up of the KK Nagar branch, he was shocked by his attitude.

'I did not like his argument at all,' Rajagopal recalled. 'If I retorted, he would silence me saying, "You don't know anything about this, be quiet." The only option was to sack him.'

After giving his manager the marching orders, Rajagopal mined his own experience as a groceries trader, and with his chef decided what it would take to fulfil his 'burning desire' of running a restaurant 'which would earn a name for its excellence'. He set aside Rs 50,000 to compensate for the losses that the first restaurant at KK Nagar would incur by not compromising on the quality of raw materials over five months. From the sixth month onward, Rajagopal says in his book, he did not look back. What he spent on raw material and human resources, he made good on the number of 'plates' per table sold.

As the operation began to show profit, he began

'welfare schemes' for his staff. The decision came after a trip to the Thiruthani Murugan temple, about two hours from Chennai, in his then newly acquired second-hand Ambassador. He set off in pouring rain at night, and after a minor accident on the way, made it to the temple just as it was about to close at 10 p.m. It was later discovered that the car engine had lost a part as the vehicle sped through the darkness to reach Thiruthani before the temple gates closed.

For Rajagopal, making it to the temple despite the bad weather and surviving the mishap en route were signs that the gods were smiling on him. By the second year, as the cash register began to ring louder, Rajagopal decided he would do better by his employees. And thus began his much-praised schemes for all those who worked at Hotel Saravana Bhavan.

The slew of perks he offered those on his payroll was unprecedented. Foremost was that Saravana Bhavan paid the school fees and other expenses for the education of two children of every employee, right up to college. There was no cap on this, and the choice of school, college and stream of education was left entirely to the employee and his family. But the company insisted on making the payments directly to the institution. Rajagopal would say most of his employees were illiterate themselves and did not know the value of proper schooling. He feared they would spend the money on something else were he to give it to them.

He also paid the rent for family accommodation for his married employees; provided telephone connections at the homes of employees in managerial positions, and gave an annual travel allowance to those whose families lived back in the villages. All staff were also given, apart from uniforms, new clothes on Pongal; and under a scheme named after his mother, a sari for the brides of employees getting married. He gave a month's salary as Deepavali bonus; and all on the payroll got medical treatment under the ESI scheme, with the company picking up the employee's contribution. It was an in-house rule that if a family member of an employee fell sick and was hospitalized, two staffers would be deputed to look after the patient; and tiffin carriers would be delivered to the hospital with food from the Saravana kitchen three times a day. Treatment charges for employees admitted in private hospitals were also borne by Saravana Bhavan. The company paid for Life Insurance Corporation policies from Rs 50,000 up to Rs 1 lakh for all staffers. Rajagopal threw in incentives such as gold chains and gold rings, TVs, fridges, trips to Singapore; pensions for the parents of employees; and vehicles – cycles, mopeds and jeeps – for employees.

Perks like these were unheard of in any private sector job at the time, not to speak of the restaurant business with its poorly paid workers. Rajagopal thought each of these measures as necessary in themselves, first because they had been ordained by the god that he believed in, and second as something that would keep attrition down and keep the door to Saravana Bhavan from becoming a revolving door of exits and new entries.

'Rajagopal understood that the first capital is the money that we put in. The next capital is the people whom you train and invest in,' says Mahadevan.

It was smart thinking, and it left a lasting impression of Rajagopal as a do-gooder and a philanthropist, especially among his staff, even after the unsavoury side to his character came into the public eye.

The food industry average employee cost is 18 per cent to 21 per cent, Mahadevan said. 'In Annachi's case, even back in the nineties, it was 35 per cent to 36 per cent.'

Rajagopal's accountants advised him once to switch off the generosity because of the high cost of these perks. At the peak of its success, Saravana Bhavan had 6000 employees.

'They told him to end the practice at least for the new hires, but he would not listen,' Mahadevan recalled.

'It was pay not according to the nature of one's job, but according to one's needs', Rajagopal wrote. He also did away with what was then a common cost-cutting practice in the restaurant business – employing people for the short term, laying them off and then rehiring them. 'Not only that, we saw to it that there were no periodic breaks in their service. We removed the words "periodic breaks in employee's service" from our dictionary of hotel management. As the employees were given good salary in our hotels, and as there were no deliberate, periodic cuts in an employee's service, many came seeking jobs in our hotels.'

That is how a family from a remote corner of Tamil Nadu decided to sell everything they had and move to what was then Madras, to live in a welfare state called Saravana Bhavan. If they knew there was a seamier side to Rajagopal, they did not think they would get entangled in it so badly that their lives would change forever.

5

Vedaranyam is a small coastal town in Tamil Nadu, closer to Jaffna in northern Sri Lanka than to Chennai. Shaped like a nose, it juts out into Palk Strait. It was once famous as the place where C. Rajagopalachari (Rajaji) ended his salt march in April 1930, in tandem with Gandhi's Dandi March on the Gujarat coast. But in the late 1980s and early 1990s, it was better known as a favoured safe haven for Tamil Tiger cadres. They would land their speedboats on the beaches, bringing their injured for treatment in the nearby hospitals, taking back fuel and other supplies as they fought the Indian Peace-Keeping Force, and later the Sri Lankan Army, in their battle for an independent Tamil Eelam. The assassination of Rajiv Gandhi in May 1991 by a suicide bomber of the Liberation Tigers of Tamil Eelam at Sriperumbudur on the outskirts of Chennai added to Vedaranyam's notoriety as a safe haven for Sri Lankan Tamil militants. Each militant group had an office, and the 'boys' moved around freely, locals recall. After the suicide bombing, the police clamped down and the comings and goings of the militants became clandestine.

Even after all these years, Vedaranyam retains a land's-end kind of mystique. Velankani Church, an important pilgrimage spot, is some 25 kilometres north of Vedaranyam, nearer the district headquarters of Nagapattinam. Point Calimere, at the tip of the nose, has now emerged as a birders' favourite, with thousands of migrating flamingos flocking to the waters there in December. With plenty of blackbuck too, the area was declared a wildlife and bird sanctuary back in the 1960s. But in the last decade of the twentieth century, tourism in Vedaranyam was unknown, and the main occupation there was salt-making and, to a lesser extent, agriculture. If the place looked more prosperous than many others in southern Tamil Nadu, it was because of its multifaceted links, some legit and some not so legit, beyond Indian shores. Vedaranyam's NRIs, its fugitive

Sri Lankan militants, its local smugglers and fishermen, all were tied together in a loose economic quid pro quo from which everyone benefited.

~

In the mid-1990s, among those trying to make a decent living in Vedaranyam was the Malaysia-born Ramasamy. In the years before and after the Second World War, there had been a wave of migrations from Nagapattinam to Malaysia, of people setting out to work as indentured labour on the plantations. Vedaranyam was a catchment area for such workers. An old-timer recalled that families were given Rs 5 for each man they were ready to send off. A newly indentured worker's kit was a new dhoti and vest as he got into the boat. Some of these workers would go on to join the Indian National Army in Malaya. Even today, local people have strong kinship links in Malaysia, Singapore and Sri Lanka. Along the narrow winding highway to Vedaranyam from Nagapattinam, those continuing links, and the relative prosperity they have brought to the people of the area, are visible in the swish houses that line both sides of the highway.

Ramasamy's parents were part of that early wave of migration, later returning to the hamlet of Mavadivaikkal in Vedaranyam. Thanks to their Malaysia roots, they were one of the well-off families of that area. Then came the prawn farming boom of the early 1990s, which affected the groundwater in the area. The prawn hatcheries were set up in what was until then agricultural land cut into large tanks, filled with seawater and seeded with prawn, rendering the land unfit for anything else. It affected livelihoods in the area in a big way.

Ramasamy moved his family, first from the hamlet of Mavadivaikkal to the hamlet of Kallimedu. By then he had already made a foray into Chennai to look for another source of livelihood, and through a cousin called Dakshinamoorthy he found a job at Saravana Bhavan's KK Nagar branch. Soon he decided to move his entire family to the big city. In 1994, Ramasamy and his wife, Thavamani, decided to sell their house in Kallimedu, and moved with their two children, daughter Jeevajothi and son Ramkumar, to Chennai. Their move was not unusual for its time. They were among the hundreds of thousands from across rural Tamil Nadu who were heading to the cities, where the effects of the 1991 opening up of the economy were just becoming visible. From the sale of their property, the young couple had made the not insubstantial sum of Rs 7.5 lakh. They settled a debt of Rs 3 lakh in the village. The balance was still good enough to secure a good future for their children and a comfortable life in the big city. Their hopes of achieving this were entirely pinned on P. Rajagopal, the owner of Saravana Bhavan, the burgeoning restaurant chain that had already taken Chennai by storm.

Again, it was on Dakshinamoorthy's advice that Ramasamy deposited all his money with Rajagopal, who would give him an interest payment of Rs 6000 to Rs 7000 per month. It was all too good to be true. It was an unbeatable offer, better than the average 10–11 per cent interest banks then offered on term deposits. Within a couple of months, Ramasamy was also appointed as assistant manager at the Ashok Nagar Saravana Bhavan outlet, and the family was allotted a place to stay in KK Nagar, rent-free.

~

Two years went by quickly. Jeevajothi was fifteen years old. She had grown up to become a pretty teenager.

Across India, there is a racist bias in favour of light skin tones. A 'fair' or light complexion is seen as a marker of beauty, though what is 'fair' is relative, and differs from place to place. With a skin tone that met the Tamil standard of 'fair', Jeevajothi, with her large, expressive eyes and thick, curly hair, was a head-turner. It is unclear when she dropped out of school – she was too young to have completed class 10 when the family moved from Vedaranyam. But after arriving in Chennai, the parents' priority was to educate the boy.

Younger than his sister by a couple of years, Ramkumar, who was studying for his matriculation by 1996, was struggling with mathematics, and the parents hired a tutor for him. The tutor was Prince Santhakumar, a Christian from Madurai. The twenty-five-year-old had a postgraduate degree in mathematics from American College, Madurai, a prestigious institution. It was established in the nineteenth century by American Protestant missionaries, and studying there had helped many in the region find their feet in the wider world. Prince was the third in a family of five brothers and a sister, all of them well educated. He also had a regular day job as a teacher in a school. Neatly dressed, educated and confident, Prince impressed the family. Ramkumar's maths scores began to improve too.

By now Rajagopal had started taking extraordinary interest in the family, and seemed to have an outsized influence on the lives of Ramasamy and his wife, Thavamani.

~

Rajagopal was now in his late forties. Photographs taken at the inaugurations of his various ventures in the 1980s show a man of less than average height, his broad face framed by sideburns, a caterpillar moustache over his lips, hair parted in the middle and combed flat back, and always dressed in a white veshti and white shirt. He looks unsmiling and tense in those group pictures with his partners and others. As the years pass and his business grows, he puts on weight, his face becomes fleshier, he adds a double chin, and his hairline recedes, the black turning to grey. No one would claim Rajagopal had an arresting personality. Even after he attained fame, and later on notoriety, he would have been difficult to spot in a crowded Tamil Nadu mofussil bus stop.

But he had already earned a reputation as a sari

chaser. In 1994, according to court and police records, he had taken a second wife, Krithiga.

Bigamy is rampant in India, but it becomes a crime in the eyes of the law only if the first wife makes a police complaint. Examples abound, including in the world of celebrities, of women just putting up with their husband's second wife. So it was with Valli Ammal.

In Tamil Nadu, the practice has come to be institutionalized as *chinna veedu* – 'small house', literally translated. But the term really means second wife or mistress, and is derived from the house in which the man sets her up, likely an establishment smaller than the man's first. The late chief minister of Tamil Nadu M. Karunanidhi had two wives. At first it was only hush-hush talk that every day he divided his twenty-four hours between the main house and his chinna veedu. But during his stints as chief minister, the presence of policemen deployed on the route to the 'small house' made it clear that the rumour was true. In a sense, Karunanidhi normalized the practice. The two wives were both by his side when he undertook a hunger strike for a ceasefire in Sri Lanka in 2009. As he lay under a tent on Marina Beach, one sat by his head, the other at his feet. And he acknowledged his second wife by publicly referring to her as 'mother of my daughter'.

Despite all the praise that Rajagopal showered on Valli Ammal publicly, his confidence that he could take any woman he chose had grown in direct proportion to his restaurant chain. He had got married to Valli in 1972 as a twenty-five-year-old. From the single photograph of their wedding published in *I Set My Heart on Victory*, she must have been a teenager at the time, dressed in a silk sari, looking demurely away from the camera.

They were married soon after he opened his second grocery shop, the one in Ashok Nagar. When his uncle in Punnaiyadi wrote to Rajagopal that the family had found a suitable match for him in the nearby village of Siruthondanallur, he readily said yes. What sealed it for him was her name. Valli is the consort of Murugan, his favourite god, and he was attracted to her 'instantly', without having seen her even once.

The marriage was solemnized at the end of 1972 at Valli's village. 'No dowry. I have not got any article from my wife's house so far. I have not thought of getting anything free from anyone as I have confidence in myself, in my hard work.'

In a newly-wed Tamil couple's first-year calendar, the festivals of Deepavali and Pongal are big occasions. The couple celebrate them at the bride's parental home, where the groom is pampered, and the bride's parents shower the couple with gifts. But Rajagopal writes that he was busy with his shop and did not have time for the elaborate festivities of these two occasions, both of which were celebrated at home 'in a simple manner'.

In his autobiography he described his wife as 'God's gift to me', someone who helped him 'in achieving more and more success', and in 'safeguarding' his achievements. When he opened his first restaurant, she toiled by his side in the kitchen, making the pickles that would be served as part of the menu, roasting and grinding the spices herself.

'She was against unnecessary expenses. She had learnt that one should spend within one's means. She is the symbol of economy,' he said about her. Valli Ammal wore the clothes that he chose and bought for her, never asking him for anything. She was the mother of his two sons, Shiva Kumaar and Saravanan. Rajagopal was an absentee father, too preoccupied with running his shops and, later, the restaurants. She would not bother him even when the boys fell ill, taking them to the hospital by bus on her own.

He wrote, 'My soul is satisfied I have such a noble woman as a wife.'

But even if the soul was satisfied, clearly the flesh was not. Even as he was writing those lines his predatory eye had fallen on another woman. Krithiga was the wife of a chef in Saravana Bhavan. The chef, Ganesh Iyer, was a Brahmin. With Rajagopal keen to make his food to the taste of Tamil Brahmins, the man had been hired to make sweets and savoury snacks, especially Brahmin favourites such as 'murukku', which has to be twisted into shape by hand just as the dough is dropped into boiling oil. From photographs, Krithiga appears to have been in her twenties at the time of her marriage to Rajagopal. Krithiga and her husband had tried to resist the boss's advances. But Ganesh was threatened, paid off, and asked to get out. As the court records state, the murukku maker decided to take the money and do as he was told. And so did Krithiga. She and Ganesh had been married for just a year. For some time after they were thus forcefully separated – it is not clear if they divorced – Ganesh worked in an eatery in Tindivanam, a town 142 kilometres from Chennai. His brother would later depose in court as a prosecution witness, relating how Rajagopal had destroyed Ganesh's life.

Krithiga was at first a reluctant second wife, but surrendered to life with Rajagopal, perhaps because she had no choice. It was a life with no shortages, and she lived in comfort. He would say later that he 'keeps her in a Taj Mahal' with all the comforts that money could buy. He bought her a house in Ashok Nagar. In a rare photograph, she is seen with Rajagopal by her side at a ceremonial lunch at a religious function.

Valli Ammal made her peace with this marriage. She would appear at Rajagopal's side for formal functions, especially at temples, but for all practical purposes she lived separately with their two sons in KK Nagar, while Rajagopal moved in with Krithiga at Ashok Nagar.

No one could tell me where Krithiga lives now. Sometime in 2015, with Rajagopal's sons by Valli Ammal now adults managing the Saravana Bhavan chain and with families of their own, Krithiga began to worry about her future. All the signs were that she had outstayed her welcome. She decided to leave Rajagopal and his 'Taj Mahal'. And Rajagopal allowed her to go. According to a trusted former manager of Saravana

Bhavan, Rajagopal 'settled her honourably', ensuring she would not lack for anything in the foreseeable future.

~

Within just a couple of years of his marriage to Krithiga, it appears that Rajagopal's attention had moved to Jeevajothi. It was around then that he made it known to Thavamani and Ramasamy that he did not approve of Prince Santhakumar and did not want him visiting their place. They tried reasoning with him that Ramkumar's maths scores in school had improved with Prince's help. But Rajagopal was insistent: 'You have a daughter who is growing up. Get rid of the tutor,' he told Thavamani.

Ramasamy and Thavamani pushed back. They refused to discontinue Prince's services as a private tutor to their son. Rajagopal asked them to vacate the rent-free house he had given them. The family moved to a rented place in MGR Nagar, a densely packed poor settlement in the neighbourhood of KK Nagar. It was a comedown for the family. But they had made their choice.

With the souring of the relationship, Ramasamy

took back the money he had deposited with Rajagopal, though he did not get all of it back, quit his job at Saravana Bhavan and decided he would try his luck in the transport business. Ramasamy bought a truck, but he had no experience in the business and, after stacking up losses, decided to return to Malaysia to try his luck there, leaving his wife and children in Chennai.

～

By then it was 1998, four years since the family had arrived in Chennai and Rajagopal had entered their lives. It had become clear that Rajagopal's interest in the family went beyond that of an employer keeping track of the well-being of an employee. He kept in touch with Thavamani even after Ramasamy quit Saravana Bhavan and the family had left the house that came with his job. It was almost as if Rajagopal had appointed himself a guardian of the family, but with intentions that were far from guardian-like. At this stage, Thavamani did nothing to discourage Rajagopal. As it became apparent by and by, the family had entered into too many transactions with Rajagopal to make a complete break from him.

Prince had been a tutor to Ramkumar for over two years, and in that role remained a frequent visitor to the small MGR Nagar house where the family now lived. He and Jeevajothi fell in love. Thavamani was aghast when she found out. Her daughter, she declared, was not going to marry a Christian. But Jeevajothi was not going to let her mother come in the way of her plans.

On 28 April 1999, Jeevajothi, then eighteen years old, slipped out of the house and met up with Prince. They went to the sub-registrar's office in Anna Nagar, where they got married. One of Prince's brothers, John Chelladurai, was the witness. Next, the newly-wed couple travelled to Madurai, to Prince's family home. The reception there was anything but warm. Victor, Prince's eldest brother, a pastor, asked for Jeevajothi's parents' phone number. 'Since we did not know this girl, I told Prince that I would like to inform the girl's mother formally. I asked for the mother's telephone number, and informed her,' he would tell the court years later.

The next few days went by in a haze. Thavamani and Ramkumar hotfooted it to Madurai. Reluctantly, Thavamani accepted the fait accompli. She, her son and the newly-weds returned to Chennai, where

Thavamani took them to the Marundeeswarar temple in Thiruvanmiyur in South Chennai and got their wedding solemnized by a Hindu priest in the presence of a few close relatives.

The young couple moved to Kottivakkam, then an up-and-coming neighbourhood in South Chennai, close to the sea. It was a much better area than MGR Colony. The coastline-hugging East Coast Road that now goes past Kottivakkam on its way out of Chennai towards Pondicherry had not yet been made, but where this scenic highway would later be cut, colonies of houses and shops had sprung up haphazardly. Thavamani and Ramkumar also moved out of MGR Colony and found a place close to Jeevajothi and Prince, who had by then given up his work as a teacher and become an agent for the Life Insurance Corporation of India (LIC).

Jeevajothi began to work at SS Annamalai, a small travel agency close to her home. On the surface, she and Prince were like many other young married couples at the turn of the century in liberalized India, trying to keep up with a booming consumer life, with aspirations that seemed within reach, provided you were ready for the hard slog.

But beneath their seemingly humdrum life in Kottivakkam, nothing was going right for Jeevajothi and Prince.

The nightmare really began to unfold in one horrific episode after another with Jeevajothi's decision to start her own travel agency in early 2001. She had two years' experience in the field. Prince had already given up his LIC job to help her with the business. What else did they need? Money.

~

Loans those days were not easy – as indeed they are not today – for those who did not have money already. A man like Rajagopal could swing bank loans even back in the 1980s, when public sector banks were tight-fisted, because he and his restaurants were well known. Also, a bank manager with the Indian Bank – who was convicted in 2019 for a bank fraud, one of several corruption investigations against him – was well disposed towards Rajagopal. Even in liberalized 2001 India, if you were a new entrepreneur with no track record, and with no family wealth or influence, convincing a bank to lend you money was like climbing Everest without oxygen. People gave up at 16,000 feet. Most just borrowed small amounts from friends or family, who parted with those sums on a wing and a prayer that they would be repaid some day.

Jeevajothi would tell the court later:

My mother borrowed [Rs] 1 lakh from [her brother] Uncle Mani. With that, we began Global Air Travels . . . When I needed additional funds, my husband tried to raise a loan from banks with the help of his friends. Since banks wanted surety, and we did not have anything to offer as collateral, the loan did not materialize. Again, I went back to my mom and asked her if she could arrange some more money. My mother said, 'I don't know anybody else. I will go to Rajagopal and try to organize some funds.' First, I heard from my mother that Rajagopal himself would provide the surety for a bank loan. Next, my mother called again to tell that Rajagopal had called her and said why go to a bank, he would lend me the money himself.

Jeevajothi, despite the alarm bells that were probably ringing in her head, decided she would take the money.

In that instant, it was as if she had opened the door to a poisonous snake that would sting her, her husband and other family members repeatedly. But unquestionably, Prince, whom Rajagopal saw as the main obstacle to his plans of marrying Jeevajothi, was the snake's main target.

6

Here's a counterfactual: had social media existed in 2001, with its hashtags and viral videos, would the powerful Pitchai Rajagopal have managed to get away with his single-minded sexual pursuit of a former employee's daughter for over half a decade? More pertinently, could a murder have been averted had Jeevajothi been able to splash her story over Facebook or Twitter? Perhaps. Perhaps not. After all, the #MeToo movement in India has largely remained confined to English-speaking professional women in big cities. Jeevajothi was facing up to Rajagopal in 2001, at a time when there was no Twitter, Insta or WhatsApp. Even mobile phones were only two or three years old in India, and Google had not yet been invented. Back then, for a twenty-something woman determined to fight off a predatory male, it meant almost a hand-to-hand combat for self-protection and self-preservation. And that, in essence, was how it was for Jeevajothi too.

By the middle of 2001, Rajagopal had become brazenly open and persistent in his determination to prise Jeevajothi away from Prince and take her as his third wife, his second chinna veedu.

An astrologer, identified in police records as Ravi of Madipakkam, a Chennai suburb, had told Rajagopal that his horoscope matched with Jeevajothi's, and marrying her would take him to the pinnacle of his achievements. That is what Rajagopal would later tell the police. For him, this prediction was further confirmation, if any was needed, that taking Jeevajothi as his third wife was predestined. It was written in his stars, and it was astrological forces that pushed him to act in his pursuit of her. Police investigators, of course, dismiss this theory – to them the astrologer was also a 'victim' of Rajagopal's machinations to acquire Jeevajothi. According to the police, even Rajagopal's first wife, Valli Ammal, appeared to sense this.

After the police caught up with Rajagopal, Assistant Commissioner of Police (ACP) K. Ramachandran, who was in charge of three Chennai police stations that were involved in the Prince Santhakumar murder investigation – Velachery, Nandanam and Guindy – had occasion to meet Valli Ammal.

'She had a request. She said to me: "Look, I know that he is a *penn pittal* [womanizer]. But thousands of livelihoods are dependent on him. He's like a big banyan tree. Please allow him to come out on bail."'

Rajagopal's sons were grown up by then, and the elder one, Shiva Kumaar, who had studied hotel management in Switzerland, was looking after the Dubai outlet of Saravana Bhavan, the restaurant's first, and at that time the only, international franchise. In 2002, when Rajagopal's bail was cancelled, he had checked himself into Vijaya Hospital. Ramachandran went to the hospital to serve him the arrest warrant. In the hospital room, he saw Shiva Kumaar, who had apparently come to take leave of his father before going to Dubai but was engaged in an argument with him about the mess that his father's obsession with women had got them into. 'Rajagopal raised his hand as if to strike his son, and I heard him say, "I will marry as many women as I like, it's none of your business",' Ramachandran recalled.

~

Rajagopal's welfare schemes for his employees enabled him to exercise enormous power over every aspect of their lives. He revelled in this power – and had already demonstrated this by brutally forcing his cook Ganesh Iyer to surrender his wife Krithiga to him. Now, it was as if his conquest of Krithiga had whetted his appetite and strengthened his belief that he could have any woman he wanted.

Through August of 2001, until the police caught up with him in November that year, Rajagopal's single-point plan was to instal Jeevajothi as his second chinna veedu. Jeevajothi's husband, Prince, her apparent love for him and her determination not to allow Rajagopal to break up their marriage were all coming in the way of his plans. He was clear that come what may, Jeevajothi would be married to him by the end of the year, if not before. After all, he was a man who had, as the title of his autobiography proclaimed, set his heart on victory. He was not going to be thwarted by her, and less so by her husband. He was not going to take no for an answer. If Prince was in the way, then too bad for Prince, he had to go. That is how Rajagopal seemed to have seen it. And that is how what began as an obsession in 1996 led to a cold-blooded murder in 2001.

~

The loan to Jeevajothi for her travel agency gave Rajagopal the opening he had been lying in wait for. He was more than eager to advance her the money, but there was a condition – the borrowers would have to go through a rite of passage.

Vellore, 138 kilometres west of Chennai, was home to Rajagopal's guru, Swami Kirubananda Variyar, a well-known Saivite preacher with a wide following across Tamil Nadu. The clean-shaven bald-headed holy man, always pictured with holy ash smeared liberally across his forehead, lots of rudraksha beads around his neck, and a broad smile across his face, much like a happy emoji, had passed away in 1994, at a time when Rajagopal's restaurant chain was taking off into the big league. But through the 1980s and earlier, it was Swami Kirubananda Variyar that the entrepreneur turned to for spiritual guidance from time to time. Variyar, whose lectures he began attending in the 1970s, inaugurated the first building that Rajagopal put up in 1976. He also inaugurated some branches of Saravana Bhavan. And it was Variyar, according to Rajagopal, who helped him understand why he was suddenly rich.

'Variyar Swamigal used to say often, "God does not give money to all, because many do not know how to spend it wisely. They will waste it, squander it. That is why God gives the owner of a business a lot of money, and makes him pay salary to his employees, whenever necessary." I took a lesson from what Variyar said. I realized that God gives me the salaries of many employees in total. I distribute them among my employees according to some well-regulated rules,' he wrote in his book. Had he heeded Variyar's advice in his personal life too, perhaps Rajagopal might have written a better ending to his own story. According to an insider, before his second marriage, Rajagopal had sought Variyar's blessings. The old man had hinted that he did not approve of the alliance. Rajagopal bowed before him and repeated: 'Your blessings please.'

After the Swami's death, Rajagopal poured money into building a *mani mandapam*, a kind of temple-cum-tomb for his spiritual guide in a place called Kangeyanallur, a small hamlet on the banks of the river Palar in Vellore. This is where Variyar was born and where he died too. His family home is a few steps away. Rajagopal located the mani mandapam at the site where the Swami was buried, in accordance with samadhi rites. Directly opposite, its entrance facing that of the mani mandapam, is a Subramanian Swamy or Murugan temple. According to an inscription at its entrance, Rajagopal and 4000 Saravana employees helped restore the temple. A mid-sized gopuram, a temple tower, soars over the entrance.

Inside the Variyar complex, a hexagonal sanctum encloses a life-sized seated idol of the Swami next to his samadhi site. A smaller idol, used for taking out in processions, is seated in front. The walls are pink, the floors are expensive granite. A large compound next to it is rented out to the public for weddings or other functions. Interlocking red and grey paver tiles make a neat pathway to a double-storeyed guest house behind the temple.

It was here that the next sad episodes in Jeevajothi's life would play out over a month and a half.

~

Rajagopal told Jeevajothi that she would have to travel to Vellore on five consecutive Fridays and offer prayers to the departed Swami at the mani mandapam. He told Thavamani that this was the correct and most appropriate way to launch a new venture. And, he added, that is where he would give Jeevajothi the money.

'I went with my family there every Friday for five weeks,' Jeevajothi recalled. 'Every time, we stayed in his guest house there.'

The guest house had seven large rooms, some equipped with air conditioners. Rajagopal always stayed in the bedroom next to the lift, which was for his use alone.

It is not clear from police records or from Jeevajothi's deposition what transpired at the guest house, what quid pro quo was forced on her for the loan. Every Friday that this 'ritual' took place, Rajagopal handed over some money to Jeevajothi's husband.

'The first Friday when we went, Rajagopal gave Rs 50,000 to Prince Santhakumar. In the second week, he gave another Rs 50,000 to my husband. On the fifth Friday, he gave a blank cheque for Rs 5 lakh to me. He asked me to write my name on it. I told him it's better in my husband's name, to which Rajagopal said, "I'm doing this for your father's sake, so write your name on it." I wrote my name on the cheque. We started running the agency,' Jeevajothi would say in court.

Jeevajothi's travel agency opened on 23 August 2001. Rajagopal organized the inauguration, arranged for a photographer to shoot pictures and took care of all the expenses for the event.

By then, Rajagopal had begun to believe that Jeevajothi was his. From the time Rajagopal had given Prince the first instalment of Rs 50,000, he had launched a full-on invasion of Jeevajothi's life. He called her every day, either at her home or at her office, tracked her movements, and asked her intrusive questions.

Even after she had opened her own travel agency, the place where she had earlier been working asked her to continue for a few days until they found a replacement. Every day after work, she would go and check on her own new enterprise. And every day Rajagopal was finding new ways to inveigle himself into Jeevajothi's life, from inviting himself to lunch at her home, where he declared that the house was too small and he would find her a new place, to insisting that she accept jewellery and a silk sari from him for her birthday on 5 September.

'On 1 September, he showed up at my place with a set of gold bangles and clothes, and gave them to me as gifts for my birthday. I asked him why he was giving me all this, when I had told him his blessings were sufficient. He said, "I have brought it, you better accept it now." He was angry that I was refusing to take it,' Jeevajothi would tell the court.

But her real trauma was yet to begin. It started on 20 September with a bizarre scene in the premises of a well-known hospital in South Chennai – Malar in Adyar. Prince had taken Jeevajothi there after she complained of feeling unwell. While she was admitted at the hospital for tests, Rajagopal strutted in with a doctor of his own in tow, with several henchmen following behind. That was another thing about Rajagopal. He never went anywhere without five or six men, all dressed in dark safari suits, apparently managers and assistant managers at his restaurants, but with the demeanour of bouncers, security guards and goons. Without permission from the attending doctor, the doctor Rajagopal brought – identified in police records as Dr Raja – studied her case sheet, declared she was being administered the wrong medicines and recommended that she be moved to another hospital.

After the doctor left, Rajagopal stayed on in the room to have a packed lunch that was sent up from his car. Jeevajothi was discharged the next day, with Rajagopal sending Rs 10,000 through two of his bouncer-henchmen for the settlement of bills. He also sent her a mobile phone. As soon as one of the henchmen handed it over to her, she received a call on it from Rajagopal, who said this phone would be his hotline to her. He would speak to her only on this phone from now on. As instructed by Rajagopal and Dr Raja, who ran a small nursing home in Ashok Nagar, Prince and Thavamani took Jeevajothi to Vijaya Hospital in Vadapalani. There, even as a woman doctor was examining Jeevajothi, Dr Raja phoned the doctor. Immediately after the call, the doctor told Jeevajothi there was nothing wrong with her and that she could go home, but her husband needed to come in for a semen test after four days. Meanwhile, the doctor instructed, the two were not to have sex.

As Jeevajothi and Prince tried to process all that was happening, there was no respite from Rajagopal. In the middle of the night once, he called Jeevajothi on the mobile phone he had given her. He said he had called to remind her of the doctor's instruction: no sex with

Prince. Four days later, on 25 September, a Saravana Bhavan bouncer arrived on a bike to take Prince to Dr Raja's clinic in Ashok Nagar. After examining him, the doctor told Prince he may be HIV-positive and would need to undergo an ELISA test. Prince refused to take the test and went back home.

The next day began ominously. Rajagopal called Jeevajothi while she was at work and boasted that he had known her husband would refuse to take an 'AIDS test'. First, he said, Prince had HIV, then he told her that Prince had given her some black-magic herbs and hormones to fill up her figure and make her look 'glamorous', and that this was why she had fallen ill. Prince's motivation for doing this, according to Rajagopal, was to make money off her. 'Glamorous' in the Tamil film industry is a euphemism for sexy, and Rajagopal claimed Prince had approached several film directors to push her into the movies.

Rajagopal's rant was more than Jeevajothi could take. She screamed at him, asking him not to interfere in her life, and disconnected the phone. Not one to be deterred, Rajagopal called again. She again shouted at him to leave her alone and cut the call. But there was no cutting off Rajagopal.

Some time after midnight, there was a knock on their door. Prince went to check who had come to their house so late. Standing at the door were Rajagopal, Jeevajothi's parents – her father had by now returned from Malaysia, having failed to find employment there – and Ramkumar.

'Your daughter does not know how to speak and who she is speaking to. She has no respect. I am standing here, and she has not even asked me to come in. When I talk to her on the phone, she does not respond properly and cuts the call. There are a thousand people just waiting for my call, but she disconnects my calls,' Rajagopal, according to court records, told her parents, mute spectators to the scene, fear writ large on their faces.

When Jeevajothi threatened to call the police, Rajagopal handed her his cell phone and said, 'Speak to any policeman you wish, all the police officers in Chennai know me, and I know them. None of them can touch me. I throw money at them in the way food is thrown to dogs, and they pick it up with their mouths just like dogs do, and scamper off.' He had worked himself into a towering rage; he boasted of having using the police to drive out his business partners.

Police investigators later said they had found out that Rajagopal had fallen out with Ganapathy Iyer and K. Ramanujam, his partners when he launched his first restaurant, over the division of shares and profits. They had parted bitterly. The partners had also made a police complaint then. But Rajagopal reached out to them when his troubles with the law began in the Prince Santhakumar case, if only to prevent them from testifying against him. In photographs in 2014, Ganapathy Iyer is seen seated by Rajagopal's side.

Rajagopal's boast about his close relations with the police may have been an idle one. But he did know the Tamil Nadu director general of police from 1991 to 1995, S. Sripal, well enough for the latter to write the foreword to his memoir, *I Set My Heart on Victory*. Sripal's office, facing Marina Beach, was just up the road from Saravana Bhavan's most prestigious branch, on RK Salai. He had attended the inauguration of this branch with his wife and other family members. And Rajagopal expresses his thanks to Tamil Nadu's most senior police officer for his 'advice and suggestions to me and to my co-workers', and for his 'deep interest in our establishment'. In the foreword, Sripal calls Rajagopal his 'spiritual brother' and says the book should be read by all youngsters like a textbook.

'There are very few people in the world who, ever being active mentally and physically, give shade to different kinds of people, like a banyan tree, who represent the quintessence of our philosophies, who are out and out humane. Among such people, Saravana Bhavan Annachi Rajagopal shines like a diamond,' Sripal wrote.

~

Repeatedly boasting about his clout with the police, Rajagopal continued his tirade as Jeevajothi's parents cowered. 'You don't really know me,' he threatened Jeevajothi. 'Krithiga was also stubborn, she and her husband tried to resist me like you are doing now, but she had to surrender to me. She lived with her husband only 365 days, now I have built her a Taj Mahal where she lives like a queen as my second wife.'

Rajagopal clearly had no idea that the Taj Mahal was a mausoleum, built for a dead queen; nor did his nervous and fearful audience, who just stood there silently as he continued his shouting. The only person there screaming back at him was Jeevajothi, threatening to call the police. But he continued to boast about how he had vanquished his partners with the help of the police and had managed to drive away Krithiga's husband in the same way.

Spotting Prince in the room, he barked at him. 'Just get out of here. Tell her she has to come with me as my third wife, or ask her to cooperate and live with me. You have two days to decide.' Rajagopal left on that threatening note. The date was 28 September.

Thavamani was to tell the court later: 'Rajagopal came to my place and said, "Is this the way to bring up a daughter? She screams at me like a witch when I call her. Why do you think I have been helping you so much?"' Jeevajothi's mother said she was completely shaken by Rajagopal's words that night as he first arrived at their house before dragging the family to Jeevajothi's home. 'He told me to listen up to what he had to say. "Whether or not you have understood, did you take me for a fool that I helped you so much? I want to marry your daughter. Persuade her to come with me, or throw out your son-in-law. This is your last chance."'

Throughout the saga, other than Jeevajothi, who had declared with unequivocal clarity that she did not wish to become part of Rajagopal's harem, every other member of her family seemed completely powerless to assert himself or herself in any way to prevent matters from developing further. For instance, picture this pathetic scene described in court records: Ramkumar, Jeevajothi's brother, who was with his parents when they and Rajagopal landed up at her place, was writhing on the floor at Rajagopal's feet, clutching them and begging his forgiveness. 'Please let it go, Annachi, please let it go, Annachi,' he pleaded, as the restaurateur stood with two menacing henchmen by his side, spewing rage at Jeevajothi for spurning him.

Or was there, at the back of her parents' mind, a tiny sliver of hope that Jeevajothi might indeed be better off in Rajagopal's 'Taj Mahal' and that an 'alliance' between their daughter and the dosa baron would improve their own prospects? Were they 'abettors' and not just powerless spectators? Indeed, this is what Jeevajothi would allege in her complaint to the police three weeks later.

The absence of intervention by Jeevajothi's parents at this stage would also become a significant element in the trial court's verdict, which convicted Rajagopal of culpable homicide not amounting to murder, instead of murder. It is impossible to speculate now on what the family's motivations were. Eventually, the case went up to the highest court in the country, and Thavamani, Jeevajothi's mother, remained a strong prosecution witness throughout. But what is undeniable is that over the years the family – Jeevajothi and Prince included – had become completely reliant on Rajagopal, their Annachi, to bail them out of their financial and other difficulties, despite his openly expressed lust for Jeevajothi and his attempts at browbeating her and her other family members into submitting to his will.

According to Jeevajothi's complaint to the police, Thavamani told her daughter that when she had eloped with Prince and run away to Madurai, Rajagopal had taunted her, telling her she should have accepted his suit for Jeevajothi instead, and he would have treated her 'like a rani'. So Thavamani was aware that Rajagopal had been eyeing Jeevajothi for a long time. Thavamani added that Rajagopal had even offered to have his men track down the runaway couple, beat up Prince and bring back Jeevajothi. She told her daughter that Rajagopal had reminded her of this conversation when she approached him for help to extricate Prince from imminent arrest over an unpaid debt.

When Jeevajothi's father, failing to find gainful

employment in Malaysia, returned to Chennai shortly after Jeevajothi's marriage to Prince and was without any means of livelihood, it was Rajagopal who again became the family's benefactor, giving them a loan of Rs 3 lakh and setting them up with a small grocery shop close to Kottivakkam, where the family had moved. They were deeply entangled in Rajagopal's web of money and threats, in awe of what in Chennai is approvingly described as 'money power'. They were intimidated by his muscle power as well – the goons who surrounded him, the contacts in the police he bragged about and the politicians he claimed to know.

~

From mid-September 2001, as one day hurtled into the next over the following weeks, the family went along with everything that Rajagopal meted out to them, appearing powerless to stop him. Prince was out of his depth. Nothing, certainly not his postgraduate degree in mathematics from American College in Madurai, had prepared him for such a situation. Only Jeevajothi continued to resist Rajagopal.

On 1 October, the day after Rajagopal's two-day

deadline had ended, Jeevajothi and Prince, both worn out and close to a meltdown, went to Marina Beach on his scooter, weighing their options as they walked on the sand. It seemed there was only one way out – and that was to leave Chennai. They decided to go home, pack a few things, take whatever cash they had, and ride away on their scooter.

Rajagopal had other plans.

7

When Jeevajothi and Prince returned home from Marina Beach, they found waiting at their doorstep Jeevajothi's parents, her brother, and several of Rajagopal's henchmen, among them Tamil Selvan, Daniel, Karmegham, Hussain and Kasi. These men were all Saravana Bhavan staffers. They had managerial designations, but they were part bouncers, part troubleshooters, and mainly goons. They may have joined initially to work in the restaurant, but had then earned Rajagopal's confidence enough for him to trust them to do his dirty work. The dark safari suits they wore, along the lines of VIP security guards, only made them look more thuggish.

Tamil Selvan told Jeevajothi and Prince that Annachi

was waiting, and they had come to take the couple to him. The henchmen had arrived with a carpenter, who had broken the lock on the front door of the couple's first-floor rented home. They had replaced the lock with one of their own. Jeevajothi had to ask one of the henchmen to let her into her own home to use the bathroom. One of them ordered the carpenter to open the door and told Jeevajothi not to bolt it from inside. Jeevajothi asked Prince to stand guard as she went inside. All this took a few minutes, and the henchmen were getting jittery and impatient at the delay.

Shouting at the couple for making Annachi wait, Tamil Selvan ordered the men to drag Prince down into one of the two waiting white Ambassador cars. When Jeevajothi emerged, she was escorted down to the same car as Prince, and so were her parents. The others crammed into the second car. Some goons rode alongside on two-wheelers. The motorcade headed to the middle-class neighbourhood of Ashok Nagar, in west Chennai, to a house that belonged to Saravana Bhavan's auditor Chandrashekhar and was being used as a godown for the restaurant chain.

There, in a room on the first floor was where the next scenes unfolded. Prince and Jeevajothi were locked up in the room. Some ten minutes after that, the door opened and Rajagopal walked in, followed by some of his henchmen and Chandrashekhar. Rajagopal folded up his veshti, strode up to Prince and struck him across the face, then pushed him to the floor and kicked him. His henchmen too rained blows on Prince.

'I fell at Rajagopal's feet and cried and begged him not to hurt my husband. My husband tried to pull me up on my feet saying I should not do that. At that Rajagopal shouted at Prince, "Don't touch her. I will kill you if you touch her. You have lost your rights to touch her," and so saying he held Prince by the throat with one hand, struck him across the face with the other, and pushed him to the ground,' Jeevajothi told the court in her deposition.

Rajagopal then asked the waiting henchmen to take Prince away and give him a thrashing. Jeevajothi recounted the events that followed in her court deposition:

As I was sitting in the corner and crying, Rajagopal closed the door and came close to me, folding his veshti up once again. He said, 'How far did you think you could run away from me? If I wished to, I could do anything to you right now, but I will not resort to that kind of cheap conduct. That's not what I want. I want to get married to you properly so that you will live with me as my wife number three till the end.' Chandrashekhar, who was also present, told me, 'Do as Annachi says, that is the best for you.'

After this, the henchmen dragged Jeevajothi's husband back into the room, all beaten up, and now Rajagopal addressed him: 'I asked you to scram, to leave this city. And you were trying to take her with you? You can't run away with her. I could take her as my wife right here, in front of you. Try and save her, if you can.'

He then asked his men to take the couple back to their home, and gave them another ultimatum, another deadline. 'I will give you a week's time. Think over everything carefully, decide and let me know—' was Rajagopal's parting shot.

A sudden twist in the saga came the next day. Most improbably, Daniel, the leader of the henchmen who had beaten up Prince in the godown the previous day, called Jeevajothi and apologized profusely. Even more astonishingly, he suggested she lodge a complaint with the police against Rajagopal. He even advised her not to go to the local police saying they probably would not register the complaint, suggesting instead that she go straight to the Chennai commissioner of police.

Jeevajothi later told the court:

On 1 October 2001, Daniel spoke to me and said, 'I am sorry, I am Rajagopal's coolie. Since he asked me to bring you, I had to do it. Since he asked me to beat you, I had to, I am sorry.' Because Daniel spoke to me like this, I thought he was on our side, and I confided all my woes to him and cried. Daniel also said to me that 'from the very first day he set eyes on you, Rajagopal was lusting after you. Also, he has got your horoscope, and he showed it to an astrologer, who told Rajagopal that if he marries you as a third wife, he will lead a life of riches and luxury forever. And if he has set his heart on something he will not stop to get it. He is determined to marry you.' At which I told him, 'I don't know what to do, please advise me.'

Daniel told me, 'Give a complaint to the police against Rajagopal.' To which I replied that Rajagopal had already told me that he can buy off the police. Daniel told me, 'Don't give the complaint at the local police station, they don't take any action. Directly go to Chennai commissioner and complain.

But my husband and I could not go out as the house was under watch.

~

It was only ten days later, on 12 October, that Jeevajothi and Prince found a way to give the slip to Rajagopal's men keeping a watch on them and managed to make it to the police commissioner's office, where Jeevajothi submitted a handwritten complaint running into thirty-eight pages detailing the harassment by Rajagopal and the incident of 1 October when she, Prince, her parents and brother were forcibly taken from their home to the Ashok Nagar godown where they were kept in confinement, assaulted, threatened, and asked to fall in line. In the complaint, she indicated that her parents were pressuring her to go with Rajagopal. The commissioner at the time was K. Muthukaruppan. He gave Jeevajothi a sympathetic hearing, even introducing her to another senior officer and asking her to keep in touch with him.

Jeevajothi recalled:

Same day, between 6 and 7 p.m., we went to the commissioner's office, met him. I gave the complaint and signed. After making enquiries, the police commissioner asked us to wait outside for some time. After 10 minutes, he came out and also the joint commissioner. And they told us to meet Shanmugha Rajeswaran who is in charge of Guindy. Shanmugha Rajeswaran gave us his personal number and asked us to get in touch with him if there was any need.

Shanmugha Rajeswaran was the deputy commissioner of police for Adyar, and Velachery fell in his zone.

Jeevajothi and Prince then headed back home to Velachery, but on nearing the place saw it was surrounded by Rajagopal's henchmen. In panic, Jeevajothi called Daniel, who told her to retreat immediately and find accommodation near the police commissioner's office in Egmore.

They did exactly as Daniel told them, checking into Pandian Lodge, a cheap hotel in Egmore, where they stayed for the next six days, waiting for the police to act on the complaint. Nothing happened. By then, ordered by Rajagopal, Jeevajothi's father had lodged a missing person's complaint with the police about her disappearance from their Velachery home. She came to know this through Daniel. In that week, Jeevajothi was entirely reliant on Daniel for information, not just about Rajagopal but about her own parents too. She did not consider the possibility that Daniel could be playing a double game. Over the past six days he had guided her with his advice twice and had won her confidence. With the police dragging their feet, Jeevajothi was panicked about what to do next, and wondered if she should go to the media. Daniel was now her go-to person for advice, her troubleshooter. He promised to arrange a press conference at which Jeevajothi could tell the world that the city's best-known restaurateur was forcing her to part with her husband and marry him as his third concurrent wife. But this time, a grand betrayal was in store for Jeevajothi.

On 18 October, Daniel told Jeevajothi that he had arranged a meeting for her with a reporter known to him. The meeting would take place in the evening, and Prince, not she, should go to meet him at the rendezvous point near a Sai Baba temple just before the Golden Beach resort on East Coast Road. The Chennai–Pondicherry 'scenic highway', as it was officially known, was then brand new, without the trippers that pack it now. And in the evenings, traffic there was thin. But Jeevajothi did not want to be left alone at Egmore, nor did she want Prince to go by himself to this meeting. They hired a taxi, and after arriving at the temple, as instructed by Daniel, they waited in the car.

What they were least expecting happened next. Two Ambassador cars blocked their cab, one on the side, one at the back. Two of Rajagopal's henchmen, Karmegham and Hussain, stepped out of one of the cars, armed with big knives. Then Daniel arrived in a Tata Sumo. At that instance Jeevajothi realized it had been a trap for Prince all along. 'Karmegham and Hussain were guarding the two passenger doors of our car. They were abusing us constantly. Some goons who had come along with them pulled out the driver of the taxi and started beating him,' she would tell the court.

Jeevajothi and Prince were also pulled out of the taxi, beaten and shoved into one of the Ambassadors, which took off in the direction of Chengelpet and stopped outside Chennai's airport at Meenambakkam for about ten minutes. Tamil Selvan was in the car with them. He had taken away their cell phones. After speaking on his phone to someone, Tamil Selvan signalled to the driver to start moving again. They stopped some 40 kilometres away on the highway near Chengelpet. After thirty minutes, at around 8.30 p.m., Rajagopal's Mercedes-Benz arrived at the same spot, and from it emerged Jeevajothi's mother. Crying, she told her daughter, 'Annachi is calling you to his car.' Jeevajothi refused to get out of the Ambassador, saying she would not get off without Prince. Karmegham and Hussain settled the matter by dragging her out and pushing her into the Mercedes. All this was happening on a busy highway on the outskirts of a major metropolitan city in the first year of the new millennium, and no one stopped to find out what was going on; nor did any passers-by think of calling the police.

Ramasamy was sitting in the front passenger seat alongside the driver. Rajagopal was at the back, where Jeevajothi was pushed in along with her mother. The Mercedes sped south past Chengelpet on the Grand Southern Trunk Road (GST Road), the main Chennai–Tiruchi highway. Rajagopal was holding a sheaf of papers in his hand. Now he waved it at Jeevajothi and said: 'Here's the copy of the complaint you gave. Didn't I tell you going to the police against me is futile?' It was never established who passed on to Rajagopal Jeevajothi's complaint against him to the police.

Rajagopal added, 'Your husband gave the complaint, right? Because you don't have the courage to do this kind of thing.'

'No, no, it's not his fault,' Jeevajothi protested. 'It was I who wrote the complaint. It's my handwriting. I want my husband back with me. Please forgive me.' A desperate Jeevajothi kept apologizing to Rajagopal for complaining to the police against him.

As if to reassure her, Rajagopal said Prince was following in the car behind. 'We are going to Tirunelveli, and he will also get there. You can meet him there,' he said. Tirunelveli is a 600-kilometre drive from Chennai. In 2001, Tamil Nadu did not have the expressways that it does now, and even GST Road was a slim double carriageway. They would drive through the night to their destination. Jeevajothi kept turning around to check if the Ambassador with Prince was following, but there was no sign of it. Rajagopal said the men in the Ambassador had turned around to return to Chennai to collect some cash, and after that they would drive to Tirunelveli too, to join up with them.

～

By next morning, they were in a village called Parappadi, some 45 kilometres south of Tirunelveli town, off National Highway 44. Driving past fields of paddy and churches of various denominations (it is a predominantly Christian village), they made their way straight to a hamlet called Elankulam, to the house of a seventy-three-year-old woman called Kuzhandai Pandichi. Tirunelveli district is known for its practitioners of *nattu marundu* or folk medicine, healer-diviners who claim to know secret mantras and have knowledge of medicinal herbs, passed down orally from one generation to the next in the same family. They claim they can cure people of a range of problems, from a stomach ache to an enemy's evil eye.

Rajagopal had decided that Jeevajothi needed to be 'cured of Prince'. He told Jeevajothi that she was under Prince's spell, that he had possessed her by feeding her something, and she needed to be shaken out of his spell. She would have to 'take the medicine'. In Tamil, the process is called *thokku edukkarthu*, literally, 'taking out the paste'.

It was not often that a big car drove up to the door of Pandichi's dilapidated house. As if that was not enough, a second car with Rajagopal's henchmen also drove up behind.

'Usually, it is only poor people who come to us, those who cannot afford to go to hospitals. Their kids have swallowed something, or they have a stomach ache. We give them medicine. Sometimes adults also come,' Pandichi's daughter Sornathuraichi tells me when I visit their home in December 2020. Her mother died in 2011, but Sornathuraichi, who was present when Rajagopal brought Jeevajothi to her mother, has a vivid memory of that visit nineteen years ago by the 'big man who owned a hotel'.

The procedure, if it can be called that, on Jeevajothi required the insertion of a metal tube about half an inch in diameter into her mouth as far as it would go, with the other end of this tube in Pandichi's mouth. Before the procedure, Jeevajothi was asked to drink a bottle of water. Then Pandichi chanted a mantra and sucked repeatedly into her end of the tube, like a child making guzzling sounds with a straw. After a minute or so of this, Pandichi took the pipe out and spat something, as if she had sucked something out of Jeevajothi's stomach.

'It was vomit. It was the colour of dark dirt,' says Sornathuraichi. 'I remember the big man gave my mother two hundred rupees of his own volition. Our usual charge is fifty rupees. It was fifty then, and it is fifty now. We never solicit customers. It is they who come looking for us.'

A framed photograph of Pandichi, white-haired, and wearing a white sari and white blouse against a blue background, hangs on the freshly painted pink wall of the house. When Rajagopal came to see her back in 2001, the house was not so nice, Sornathuraichi says. One of Pandichi's three daughters, Thuraichi, is a postwoman. She delivers mail on her white scooter. And now it is Pandichi's eldest daughter, Kalyani, whom people come to for treatment.

Months after Rajagopal's visit, as part of the murder investigation, the police descended on the village. 'Van after van with policemen in plain clothes, they came, and they took my mother to Chennai in a car. She went and told the court about them coming here. She was so scared, she was shaking, and she could not eat properly for months afterwards,' said Sornathuraichi.

After the 'cure', Rajagopal took Jeevajothi to another hamlet in Parappadi called Veppankulam, to a diviner called Chellammal, who played with cowrie shells and spoke to her own god to figure out why Jeevajothi was being so stubborn, and how long it would take for her to snap out of Prince's spell and surrender to Rajagopal.

Throughout these bizarre experiences, Jeevajothi could only think of her missing Prince. But there was no sign of him or of the men who had taken him away in the Ambassador. The group drove on to Tirunelveli, heading straight to Rajagopal's favourite Ariyas Hotel. Jeevajothi's brother, Ramkumar, was waiting there for them. Some of the henchmen who had taken away Prince surfaced at the hotel, but there was no Prince. After a few hours at Ariyas, the entire party – Jeevajothi, her parents, her brother, Rajagopal, and three or four of his henchmen – boarded a train back to Chennai that evening. All through the journey, Rajagopal taunted her about her complaint to the police, waving it in her face and asking: 'Who gave this complaint, hah, who gave this complaint?'

8

From here, matters moved swiftly to their violent climax. These would be the last six days of Prince's life. And the last days of Jeevajothi's hopes that somehow Rajagopal could be made to see reason, that he would let her and Prince go, that they could perhaps move to another town, start anew and build a better life together. The young couple were not to know that the end was so near for Prince. But as they woke up to a new horrific episode each morning, a new plan by Rajagopal to prise them apart, perhaps the realization had begun to dawn that there would be no happy ending to this story.

A chronology of events as they unfolded conveys the full extent of the nightmare that Rajagopal unleashed on Jeevajothi and Prince in those six days.

20 October: On returning to Chennai after the overnight train journey from Tirunelveli, one of Rajagopal's henchmen drops off Jeevajothi, her parents and her brother at their home in Ayodhya Colony, Velachery.

Prince is still missing. While they were at Vepankulam village the previous day with the woman who read cowrie shells, an employee of Rajagopal's had suddenly shown up. Janarthanam looked like he had an urgent message for his boss. They stepped aside and spoke in hushed tones. After the two men had finished whispering to each other, Janarthanam gave Jeevajothi the news that her husband had escaped from the car in which they were bringing him to meet her at this village, and his whereabouts were now unknown. The news sent Jeevajothi into shock. There were no answers to her questions.

All she can do now is pray for his safety and hope he will get in touch with her, from wherever he is.

21 October: Jeevajothi's prayers are answered. Her phone rings. It is Prince. He is alive, and unhurt. But the news he has to share is hardly good. For the first time in this tragic saga, Jeevajothi and Prince are face

114

to face with the reality that Rajagopal is prepared to kill to have his way. Prince breaks it to her: Rajagopal had given Rs 5 lakh to Daniel to kill him. That is why he was bundled into a separate car and driven away in another direction. Once again, it was Daniel to the rescue. It was his sudden twinge of – call it conscience, call it pity – that had saved Prince. Overwhelmed by the enormity of what he was about to do to Prince, Daniel let him go, but with a warning: 'Go as far away from here as you can, go to Bombay, forget about Jeevajothi, and don't think of coming back here. Don't even sleep with your pillow in the direction of Chennai.'

Prince asks Jeevajothi to escape from her home. Impossible, she says. The house is under constant surveillance: eight to ten goons keep vigil around it at all hours of day and night. She persuades Prince to come to her. She believes the two can appeal to some residual goodness that Rajagopal must have, even though there was nothing to suggest this in his dealings with them. 'We will tell Annachi about Daniel, that he is the one responsible for telling us to give a complaint and misleading us in other ways, we will beg Annachi's forgiveness.' Prince throws caution to the winds, goes to meet Jeevajothi at her parents' place in Velachery.

Jeevajothi calls Rajagopal, tells him her husband has returned and is at her place. Within minutes, Rajagopal is at Velachery. Jeevajothi and Prince fall at his feet and beg forgiveness. They tell him they will take back the police complaint. Rajagopal, as usual surrounded by his henchmen, is non-committal. He simply asks the couple to come to his Vadapalani office that evening, and strides out.

For Jeevajothi and her family, leaving the house to go anywhere, even on Rajagopal's orders to his office, is not a simple matter of going from place A to place B. Rajagopal has thrown a cordon sanitaire around them. They are under round-the-clock surveillance. They can leave only under the escort of his henchmen. At the appointed hour, two of Rajagopal's men, Tamil Selvan and Kasi, arrive at Velachery and take the family to the Saravana Bhavan office headquarters in the congested Vadapalani area, right next to the biggest Murugan temple in Chennai.

Vadapalani gets its name from Palani in south-western Tamil Nadu, close to Madurai and Kodaikanal. A famous Murugan temple on a hill there attracts pilgrims by the thousands daily. Vada is short for vadakku, the Tamil word for north, and the temple in Chennai became Murugan's abode north of Palani. Around the temple has grown a large and dense neighbourhood, with matchbox apartments and businesses and shops crammed next to each other. But Saravana Bhavan managed to find a sweet spot, next to the arch from where the driveway to the temple begins. Nothing could have been better for Rajagopal. He was next to his favourite god. The Saravana Bhavan there is now a complex of two buildings, one a glass-fronted two-storeyed office block, and opposite it the restaurant, painted in sandstone pink, with its brown faux-tiled sloping roof and its columns inside, with items on the menu such as 'dozza' – a combination of pizza and dosa.

On the floor above the restaurant is where Rajagopal's office used to be twenty years ago. That is where Jeevajothi and her family are taken.

While they remain locked up in one room, unknown to them Rajagopal is doing his own piecing together of events – with none other than Daniel, who in turn has no idea that the person he had freed some days earlier had circled his way back to the very man who wanted him killed, and was at present in the next room with Jeevajothi.

Rajagopal questions Daniel: what had he done with

Prince? Daniel gives him a detailed reply: he stripped Prince of his clothes, tied him to the railway tracks; a train had run over him, smashing his face and body beyond recognition. Then he burnt all of Prince's clothes after dousing them in petrol. A perfect murder, as there would be no clues. No face, no body, no clothes – Prince wiped off the face of the earth.

Rajagopal hears him out, nods approvingly. He signals to a henchman. The door opens, and with a dramatic flourish, Prince is dragged in, and is now face to face with the man who has just claimed to have eliminated him without a trace. Jeevajothi follows close behind, like his shadow.

'Who is this, then?' Rajagopal asks Daniel, anger and sarcasm dripping from each syllable. '[Prince] Santhakumar's elder brother, or his younger brother or his ghost?'

Aghast and terrified at being exposed as a liar to his ruthless boss, Daniel pounces on Prince and starts pummelling him with his bare hands. 'I committed a huge blunder by taking pity on you. You've humiliated me in front of Annachi,' he screams. Karmegham and Hussain join Daniel in beating up Prince.

The scene in that room, and each of the characters

peopling it, could have been straight out of a Tamil television potboiler.

Standing next to Rajagopal are his auditor Chandrashekhar, and a lawyer known as Yaanai or 'Elephant' Rajendran, because of his purported love of elephants. He claims to have been given the title by none other than Prime Minister Atal Bihari Vajpayee, whom he further claims to have met through President A.P.J. Abdul Kalam. In that room, he is no elephant hugging animal-activist but a hard-nosed lawyer whose real name is G. Rajendran. He tells Rajagopal to send the goons out of the room, and they all get down to the main agenda of the assembly – to get Jeevajothi and her family members to sign many blank sheets of paper.

'Only our family was there. Yaanai Rajendran asked Rajagopal to take our signatures on blank sheets. Mine, Prince's, and those of my other family members. Prince and I signed on two more blank sheets. They took it for the purpose of withdrawing the [October 12] police complaint,' Jeevajothi would later tell the court.

24 October: Lawyer Yaanai Rajendran and Rajagopal's henchmen Janarthanam and Kasi take Jeevajothi and her husband to Guindy police station, where Yaanai tells

ACP Ramachandran that the whole episode is a 'family matter' that has been resolved and the complainant would like to take her complaint back.

Ramachandran takes one look at Jeevajothi's crumpled face and her generally broken look. He tells them that the matter has gone to court, and it is there that they have to appeal for withdrawal.

The entire party goes to the Chennai district court. But it is no simple matter that can be done within hours or in a day. Jeevajothi and Prince are told to put their signatures again on more sheets of paper by Yaanai, and are dropped back at her parents' home in Velachery, with the instruction to be ready in the evening: Annachi had once again given 'movement orders', and the entire party was to travel by road to Tirunelveli. Again.

At 6.30 p.m., Tamil Selvan and Kasi arrive, this time in a Tata Sumo. Jeevajothi, her parents, brother and Prince are packed into it. Destination Tirunelveli. Rajagopal is travelling separately, in his Mercedes.

25 October: The first stop is Veppankulam, where Chellammal reads the cowrie shells again, and prescribes more medicine. Next, the entourage makes its way to Parappadi, where the healer-diviner Pandichi works on Jeevajothi, inserting the metal tube into her mouth again, and once again spitting out a dark substance after sucking at it from her end, as if it were a straw.

Next stop, the Murugan temple at Tiruchendur, a big pilgrimage centre by the sea, just south of Thoothukudi. The same temple in the direction of which Rajagopal had learnt to bow twice a day from his childhood, like everyone else at Punnaiyadi. After visiting the temple, they move into a temple guest house, and later to Ariyas Hotel. Rajagopal is not present, yet his shadow looms over the entire day. Tamil Selvan and Kasi say he is staying at his own place in Tiruchendur.

26 October: Tamil Selvan gives Jeevajothi and her family a wake-up call at Ariyas Hotel at 6.30 a.m. He's at the door, telling them Rajagopal wants to meet Prince. Jeevajothi follows her husband downstairs. Rajagopal asks the couple to get into the waiting Tata Sumo as he wanted to say something important to them. The car is driven away by one of Rajagopal's men. Another Tata Sumo follows behind. After a short ride of about ten to twelve minutes, both vehicles stop at the Karai Irrupu culvert.

The culvert, on the main Madurai highway, is a few

kilometres short of Tirunelveli. A hospital has now come up on one side, and a few small workshops on the other. Beyond is open grassy land as far as the eye can see, save for a few palmyra trees. On the hospital side are paddy fields, and beyond those a couple of buildings. The state highway is now a busy double carriageway, with concrete beam-breakers in the middle, but twenty years ago this would have been a desolate spot with no traffic and none of these constructions.

The group of goons on this day – Daniel, Karmegham, Hussain and Kasi – get out of the second Sumo and come up to the one in front. Rajagopal steps out, pulls Prince out by his shirt and hands him over to the four men, who bundle him into the second Sumo. Rajagopal's instructions to the men, as Jeevajothi would recount in court: Finish him off – *ivana mudichudunge*. She is overpowered by Rajagopal as she attempts to get out of the car. She does not know it then, but this would be the last time she sees Prince alive. More pertinently for the court, it would be the last time that Prince would be seen alive in the company of Rajagopal.

27 October: Rajagopal, his goons, Jeevajothi, her parents and brother return to Chennai. Jeevajothi and her family are prisoners in their own home. Rajagopal's henchmen are standing guard around it, as usual.

29/30 October: Rajagopal arranges a visit to a horoscope reader. His name is Ravi Josiyar. He reads Prince's and Jeevajothi's horoscopes and pronounces them incompatible as husband and wife. More suited as brother and sister, he declares, and predicts Prince will never come back. The Josiyar, Tamil for fortune teller, inspects Jeevajothi's chart and discovers a dosham, or a malefic, in her stars. To remedy this, she must go and see a priest in KK Nagar.

The priest Raghunatha Iyer's home is where Jeevajothi meets Krithiga, the second wife of Rajagopal, for the first time. Rajagopal is there too. The priest instructs her to go into an empty room, where she must look at her reflection in a vessel filled with oil. When she re-emerges from this room, Krithiga removes Jeevajothi's thali – the necklace that is the symbol of her marriage to Prince – and ties another one around her neck.

Back at her mother's home in Velachery, the family remain under house arrest. Jeevajothi has stopped eating. All of twenty-one years old, Jeevajothi had no idea she had been through a ritual for a woman whose husband has died. It is when she tells her mother about the ritual that Jeevajothi realizes that the priest had rushed her through what were Prince's funeral rites and a second marriage, all within a matter of minutes. She is hoping that the phone will ring, as it had less than ten days earlier, and that Prince would be at the other end. And this time, if he told her to escape and join him, she would agree. But the phone does not ring.

Jeevajothi falls into a deep depression. Alarmed at her condition, her parents decide they have to seek help. That day they step out, telling Rajagopal's thugs they have some shopping to do. As Jeevajothi and Ramkumar are still at home, the men let the parents go. From a landline in a shop, Thavamani calls her brother Dasamani in Thethakudi, their village in Vedaranyam. She explains the dire turn of events, and asks him to come to Chennai without losing any time.

6 November: Jeevajothi's maternal uncle Dasamani arrives from faraway Thethakudi. He insists that the whole family accompany him back to Vedaranyam. He knows the Dravida Munnetra Kazhagam (DMK) legislator S.K. Vedharathinam there, who is also a distant cousin. He will help sort this out, Dasamani tells his sister. He assures her that they will mount their own search operation for Prince. For the family, after months of utter helplessness and powerlessness, Dasamani's confidence has a comforting and reassuring ring to it. But Rajagopal has to be told a credible story so that he will permit them to leave. Thavamani asks Rajagopal to allow them to take Jeevajothi back to their ooru (native village) for a few days. There they will persuade her to change her mind and accept him as her husband. Rajagopal agrees.

The family departs for Vedaranyam.

9 November: Jeevajothi returns to Chennai with her parents and brother. Something has changed, and she is no longer as broken and bereft of hope.

According to one account, a team of police officers from Chennai came to Thethakudi, looking for Jeevajothi to ask for details about her 12 October complaint to the Chennai commissioner of police – the complaint she had made on Daniel's advice, about her and Prince's wrongful confinement on 1 October at the Ashok Nagar godown where Rajagopal had Prince beaten up, threatened him with death if he touched Jeevajothi, and asked him to leave the city for his own good, the same complaint that Rajagopal had brandished angrily at her. The police officers learn that a lot has changed since then. Prince is nowhere to be found. He was last seen at the Karai Irrupu culvert when Rajagopal ordered his men to take him away and 'finish him off'. The police ask Jeevajothi to return to Chennai. They are going to register an FIR on the basis of the 12 October complaint and she needs to be present to give a statement to the magistrate. The complaint, the Supreme Court would note two decades later, was referred by the police commissioner the very next day, 'with a directive to conduct a proper enquiry and take necessary action in accordance with the law', but reached the jurisdictional Velachery police station only in the first week of November. The police did not offer any explanation for this in the courts. Prince might have been alive today had the police acted with alacrity on that complaint.

With the police's sudden interest in the case, Jeevajothi summons up the confidence to return to Chennai without fear of being waylaid by Rajagopal and his goons. She is also confident enough to go to Velachery police station in south Chennai for the registration of the FIR – the same police station she had felt could not be trusted to accept her first complaint. (As mentioned earlier, it was never established how Jeevajothi's first complaint to the police landed in the hands of the very person against whom she had made it.)

Velachery is under Inspector of Police P. Deivasigamani. His superior officers would later describe him as the 'right officer' for the job. 'He is not like the others, he is bit different, very straight,' is what one senior official told me. Deivasigamani registers an FIR under Sections 120(b) – criminal conspiracy; 147 – rioting; 364 – kidnapping or abducting with intent to murder. Over the next two days, Deivasigamani questions Jeevajothi On 15 November, she also makes a statement under Section 164 of the Cr.PC before a magistrate, a procedure that gives the statement more sanctity in the eyes of the courts and makes it less vulnerable to version changes in court.

16 November: The arrests begin in the 1 October case. The first to be picked up are the chartered accountant Chandrashekhar and three henchmen.

20 November: Jeevajothi makes a second complaint at Velachery police station, alleging that Rajagopal and his accomplices have murdered her husband. A second FIR is registered under sections of the Indian Penal Code (IPC) relating to abduction with intent to murder. The section on murder would be added later, after the body is found.

22 November: Jeevajothi is taken to the metropolitan magistrate at the district courts at Egmore to record her statement. Calmly, she submits a statement detailing all the events that had taken place to the magistrate – 'in my own handwriting', she would later tell the court. The family then returns to Vedaranyam.

The police, whom Rajagopal had compared to 'dogs' who would grab the money he could throw at them 'with their mouths and scamper off', are now showing a new urgency about the case. The restaurant mogul also seems to have sensed the change in the attitude of the police, but remains confident of brazening it out; he is still not worried about being able to handle them. For too long he had been used to having his way. Jeevajothi was the only one who had refused to bend to his will.

22 November: Rajagopal's most trusted henchmen, Daniel, Karmegham, Hussain and Tamil Selvan, surrender before the judicial magistrate at Tirunelveli and are sent to Palayankottai prison.

23 November: Realizing that some of his men have been arrested already in the 1 October case, some have surrendered, and that the police are closing in on him, Rajagopal, keen to avoid arrest and a night in police custody, surrenders at the court of the judicial magistrate in Kanchipuram with his driver Muruganandam, also an accused in the case. They are sent to Madras Central Jail. Deivasigamani applies for and obtains Rajagopal's custody for five days, from 28 November.

Further evidence that the police are now paying new attention to Jeevajothi's complaint: on the same day, the police commissioner, realizing that it may be difficult for a single police officer to handle the investigation, issues an order deputing five inspectors of police to assist Deivasigamani – the heads of Kotturpuram, Kodambakkam, Saidapet police stations, a crime branch inspector, and the inspector (crime) at Velachery police station. The next day, the Chennai collector, at the request of Deputy Commissioner of Police Shanmugha Rajeswaran at Guindy, under whose supervision Velachery police station falls, deputes four revenue inspectors and two village administrative officers to assist the police during the interrogation of Rajagopal and the other accused.

It was only at the time of Rajagopal's denouement, a long eighteen years later in March 2019, that Jeevajothi came out about what might have possibly helped bring about a turn of events in her favour in the last days of November 2001. It was, claimed Jeevajothi, her meeting with another woman. That woman was no ordinary person. She had battled many odds to rise to the top, and knew what it was to be wronged by a man.

9

In May 2001, in the state assembly elections held that year, the All India Anna Dravida Munnetra Kazhagam (AIADMK), led by its supremo, J. Jayalalithaa, was voted to power. Jayalalithaa herself had been barred from contesting the elections because of her conviction in a corruption case, and she was therefore not a member of the Legislative Assembly. But she nevertheless declared that the electoral verdict meant that the people had voted for her to lead the state, and AIADMK legislators duly elected her as chief minister. In a widely criticized decision, she was sworn in as chief minister on 14 May 2001 by the Tamil Nadu governor Fathima Beevi, previously a judge in the Supreme Court. Four months later, on 21 September, the Supreme Court declared

Jayalalithaa's appointment illegal, null and void – not surprisingly, since it violated constitutional norms. Forced to step down, Jayalalithaa appointed a loyalist in her place, but unquestionably she remained the de facto chief minister. She was the one running the state, and everyone from the chief secretary to the Chennai commissioner of police, down to the last police constable, knew this.

In 2019, when the Supreme Court confirmed Rajagopal's life imprisonment for the murder of Prince Santhakumar, Jeevajothi would claim for the first time that the late AIADMK supremo – she had died in December 2016 – had come to her aid: 'It was on Amma's orders that the police investigated the case seriously,' she told TV channels. 'Had she been alive, I would have gone and fallen at her feet in gratitude, and asked for her blessings.' In a brief conversation with me, Jeevajothi repeated this claim. But except to say that Jayalalithaa was not chief minister at the time when she stood before her and beseeched her for help 'with folded hands and tears in my eyes', Jeevajothi could not provide any details, such as the date or venue, about her meeting with the leader.

As Prince disappeared at the end of October 2001,

and Jeevajothi feared he had been killed, it is probable that she met Jayalalithaa during the period when she was no longer chief minister but still very much had the reins of power in her hands.

It is also possible that the AIADMK leader may have taken an interest in the case on her own initiative after it came to her notice that a police complaint had been made by a woman against a VIP. Jayalalithaa had a record of helping women in distress. For example, in her final months in office, she sacked one of her most trusted ministers, allegedly after the minister's wife and son met her to complain about his extramarital affair. Perhaps it was because of her own experience as an actor, battling predatory male co-stars, or as a politician who had to fight hard to survive in the man's world that is politics in Tamil Nadu that she helped Jeevajothi. Jayalalithaa was once even physically manhandled by a DMK stalwart who held on to her sari as she tried to leave the House amid much violence between the MLAs of her party and the DMK's. Newspapers would compare her predicament that day to the disrobing of Draupadi in the Mahabharata.

~

Police officials dismiss Jeevajothi's claim that they only began seriously pursuing the case on Jayalalithaa's orders. But the manner in which the police swung into action from 9 November 2001, filing FIRs, deploying additional manpower to the case and getting down to the investigations without any more loss of time, was in marked contrast to the manner in which Jeevajothi's 1 October complaint had been treated. Something had truly electrified the police for them to show such will against a man with clout. Had such action come earlier, it may not have grown into a murder investigation.

But whatever spurred the police into sudden action, so eager were they to nail Rajagopal that their investigators would even use a particular passage in *I Set My Heart on Victory* as an early indication of his 'criminal bent of mind'. Rajagopal recounts in that passage how as a child he could not resist a particular halwa that his father would bring from the weekly fair at Nazareth, a small town near Punnaiyadi. 'However contentedly I ate three times a day, I had a special liking for these sweets,' he wrote.

He would wait eagerly for his father to return from the fair. But as his father would come back only late in the night, the packet of halwa would be stowed away in its wrapper until the next morning, when Mani Ammal would cut it into equal pieces and distribute it among her four children.

But Rajagopal could never wait until the morning. 'My tongue would force me to taste the halwa during the night itself.'

He would get up in the middle of the night, stealthily unwrap the halwa, take out a piece of it and wrap it back carefully in the same away – a cover-up job so neat that his mother would not know about his night-time raid when she opened the packet the next morning.

It is a stretch to characterize this childhood tale as an early sign of adult criminality – after all, which child does not have a go at the toffee jar when no one is looking? But investigators swooped on it as they gathered evidence – it was further grist to their case against Rajagopal as a man who would stop at nothing to get what he wanted.

Rajagopal was known to have plied police stations near his restaurants with food at all hours. And policemen are said to have walked in and out of various Saravana Bhavan outlets without having to pay for their meals. But for some police investigators on the case, it was Rajagopal's taunt – he had said policemen were 'like dogs', ready to 'pick up with their mouths' whatever he would throw at them – that renewed their zeal to pursue the case against him. Inspector Deivasigamani told me that ever since he heard Jeevajothi recount Rajagopal's contemptuous words about the police, he had never stepped into a Saravana Bhavan. 'Hearing those words made me really angry,' he said.

The inspector and his senior on the case, ACP Ramachandran, who was posted at Guindy, are both retired now and work as security consultants in private firms. I met Deivasigamani first in the conference room of a swanky office in T Nagar where he now works, and he took me to meet Ramachandran, who works at another organization a few kilometres away, in Alwarpet. The two retired cops are opposites – Deivasigamani is lean, balding, wears gold-rimmed glasses, speaks quietly and surely, and remembers all the details of the case; Ramachandran, the older of the two and the more voluble, is a big-built man with a shock of still-black swept-back hair. He bangs his fists on the table in front of him now and then, when he gets agitated recalling some details of the case, especially the parts where someone approached him with an offer of money, or where witnesses were made to turn hostile.

~

After Rajagopal and his henchmen surrendered on 23 November, the case cracked open quickly. The first step was to find Prince. On 30 November, the police got custody of Daniel, the main character in Rajagopal's cast of henchmen – and the one who suffered sudden pangs of conscience – bouncers and goons, seven days after their surrender.

Inspector Allal Kathan of Kotturpuram recorded his confession, in the presence of a revenue inspector and a village administrative officer. The police now knew that Prince had been murdered and his body had been dumped somewhere in Kodaikanal. The next step was to find the body. The same night, Inspector Allal Kathan left for Kodaikanal with Daniel, Rajagopal and the others in police custody.

Rajagopal, used to travelling in the comfort of his Mercedes, was now unceremoniously shoved into the back of a police jeep with his henchmen. The journey from Chennai to Kodaikanal is easily ten hours. As one drives from Chennai, the Kodaikanal road branches off from the main Dindigul–Madurai highway. The journey uphill is a gentle ascent, with thickly wooded shola forests on either side and patches of grassy slope. At night the thick vines that wind around the branches and trunks of trees and hang over the road could be mistaken for pythons. The north-east monsoon that brings rain to Tamil Nadu in the last three months of the year creates seasonal waterfalls that course down rocky channels, across the road and down the slope on the other side. The road winds up past Vazhaimalai, Punnaikadu Vadakaraiparai, Mayiladumparai, and on until Perumal Malai.

By the time the police party, and the accused with them, reached Perumal Malai, it was the morning of 1 December. Some distance past the town, which was just then coming to life, beyond the forest checkpoint, past the rock-faced hills covered with gigantic ferns, Daniel pointed out the place where he and the others had dumped Prince's body. The spot is between Perumal Malai and Kodaikanal, in an opening where two ridges meet and a spring gushes some 70–75 metres below. Prince's body may perhaps never have been found, or never been identified, had it slipped into those fast-moving waters from the Silver Cascade waterfall. The police records mention a signboard near the spot that said 'Tiger Cholai'. The police team got out of the jeep, stepped over the low parapet gingerly, and searched through the leafy mulch for a body. Not finding anything resembling the remains of a human being, they headed to the Kodaikanal police station.

There it was as if two lost pieces of a jigsaw puzzle had suddenly found each other. The Chennai team said they were looking for a body. The Kodai police told the visiting police party from Chennai about the unidentified male body that had been found on 31 October at exactly the spot where they had been searching for Prince. They also told the Chennai team that they had given the body a burial. For a small police station, the police officers posted in Kodai had done a professional job of retaining everything that they had found on the body. Importantly, they had taken photographs of the body – eight in all.

Now, with Rajagopal, Daniel and the others in front of them, the Kodai police produced the photographs, and the clothes that Prince was wearing when his body was found. Meanwhile, someone in the Chennai police team called Jeevajothi's uncle Dasamani and asked him to bring over Jeevajothi and her family.

'So I, with my uncle, parents and brother, we all left for Kodaikanal, and got there on 2 December. We arrived at the police station around 12 noon. I was shown a blue-coloured full-sleeved checked shirt, and sandal-coloured jeans, and a black belt. The shirt was the one he was wearing when I last saw him. They asked us to stay on there for a couple of more days. On 4 December, they took me to the spot where the body was buried,' Jeevajothi would tell the court.

Jeevajothi was present as Prince's body was exhumed at nine-thirty that morning. Exhuming a body for a criminal investigation is a huge process. It needs all kinds of permissions, from the district administration, the municipal corporation, the local police. A full medical team of Dr Meiyazhagan, the district police surgeon and professor of forensic medicine at Madurai Medical College, Natarajan, an assistant professor of forensic medicine from the same college, and Chandran, a typist, were present. Before Prince's body had been buried, a post-mortem had been conducted. Now, a second post-mortem would be conducted, on the spot.

Apart from all the identity matches that had already

been made from the photographs, Jeevajothi, shell-shocked, identified the body of her dead husband by a scar on his right hip. Finding the body and confirming its identity constituted a huge breakthrough in the police investigation.

'You must have seen Kodaikanal, or any of these other hill stations. When someone tells you they have thrown a body down a hill, it could mean two thousand feet or three thousand feet. We have all seen such scenes in the movies. It rolls all the way down. In this case, it was Rajagopal's bad luck and our good fortune that the body's fall was broken within fifteen or twenty feet. A rock projection on the hill slope had stopped the body from going any further,' said Delvasigamani.

On 12 December, in the same way that Daniel had led Inspector Allal Kathan to Kodai, Rajagopal took Inspector Deivasigamani to each of the places where he had taken Jeevajothi and her family: the villages where shamans and diviners used their so-called magical powers to drive Prince out of Jeevajothi's mind; the Tiruchendur temple guest house; and Ariyas Hotel. Rajagopal also took Inspector Deivasigamani to the Karai Irrupu culvert, where the two cars that had left Ariyas Hotel on the morning of 26 October – one with

Rajagopal, Jeevajothi, Prince and Tamil Selvan, and the other with Daniel, Hussain, Karmegham and Kasi – had stopped; where Rajagopal had pulled Prince out of his car and asked the others to take him away and finish him off.

The cloth with which Prince was strangulated was found in the house of one of the goons, along with two of Prince's belongings: a gold chain and a wallet containing a couple of thousand rupees and a passport photo of Jeevajothi in its plastic display pocket.

10

Two years would pass before the trial in the Prince Santhakumar murder case began in a special court at Poonamallee, on the outskirts of Chennai. Under a Supreme Court directive in 2001, these special fast-track courts were being set up across the country to dispose of a huge backlog of cases, and in Tamil Nadu forty-nine such courts had been created. The Poonamallee court was one of them.

The charge sheet in the case had been filed in February 2002. The case had been transferred from the Chennai sessions court to Poonamallee in January 2003. There were nine accused. Rajagopal, fifty-five years old at the time, by then a celebrated restaurateur with a rags-to-riches story and a golden line in dosas, was

Accused Number 1. Daniel, his right-hand henchman, was Accused Number 2. Karmegham, Hussain, Tamil Selvan, Kasi, Pattu Rajan, Sethu, Muruganandam, followed in that order. All were charged under sections of the Indian Penal Code relating to the offences of abduction, murder and conspiracy. The prosecution listed forty-two witnesses and 121 exhibits, including documents, and seventy-nine material objects.

The court, inside a camp of the paramilitary Central Reserve Police Force 29 kilometres outside Chennai, had been originally set up there for the Rajiv Gandhi assassination trial. Its campus housed a sub-jail where the assassination accused were locked up during their trial, which continued through most of the 1990s.

At the time the court case against Rajagopal and the other accused began in 2003, the other person being tried there was Vaiko, leader of the Malumaraichi Dravida Munnetra Kazhagam (MDMK). Chief Minister Jayalalithaa had had him arrested under the draconian Prevention of Terrorism Act (POTA) for making a speech in favour of the Tamil Tigers. The *Hindu* reporter R.K. Radhakrishnan, who was covering the Vaiko trial, recalls running into Rajagopal a couple of times: 'I used to see him standing outside, meeting his employees, holding court with them, running his business while the trial was going on inside. He did not seem too keen about following what was being said about him inside the courtroom.'

On one of those days, Radhakrishnan struck up a conversation with Rajagopal. 'He was very confident that nothing would happen to him. "All this is nothing," is what he told me,' Radhakrishnan said, recalling a man who might have seen his troubles with the law then as nothing more than a short interruption in his grand plans.

They had certainly not interrupted Saravana Bhavan's massive expansion at home and abroad. The first of the chain's international outlets to come up was in Dubai, with its huge Indian expatriate population. That was in 2000, at a time when Rajagopal was nursing his obsession with Jeevajothi, planning and plotting ways to get her husband, Prince, out of the way. As his trial progressed, his restaurant empire would continue to grow.

~

Rajagopal had been out on bail since 27 February 2002. The sessions court had first granted him 'default bail' on the grounds (under provisions in the Code of Criminal Procedure) that the charge sheet had been filed late, after the stipulated deadline of ninety days from the date of taking the accused into custody. On 1 April 2002, the Madras High Court struck down the default bail, but granted Rajagopal regular bail.

There was a condition, however: Rajagopal must stay for two months in Cuddalore, a coastal town 188 kilometres south of Chennai beyond Pondicherry, and report to the police station there every day. But puzzlingly, within days the court modified the condition, bringing him closer to Chennai. Rajagopal could now stay for those two months at Kanchipuram, just 75 kilometres from Chennai, and report to the police station there.

By then, Saravana Bhavan was a byword in Kanchipuram, with three flourishing outlets in the temple-cum-sari town. The pontiff of the Kanchi Kamakoti Mutt, Jayendra Saraswati, had participated in the opening puja for the first outlet in 1991. For Rajagopal, it was as good as a homecoming.

Pilgrims who headed to this part of the country had a well-chalked-out temple trail: first to Tirupati in Andhra Pradesh for a nanosecond glimpse of Lord

Venkateswara (that is all that was possible in the crush of fellow worshippers) after tonsuring their heads and giving their hair as an offering to the god; then hop back into the bus to the next destination, Tiruchanur. From there to Sri Kalahasti and Chennai, followed by Kanchipuram with its magnificent Pallava period temples to Shiva and Vishnu, and its hundreds of shops selling silk saris and veshtis; and finally, to Mahabalipuram. It was a sort of golden triangle of temples, sari safaris and beaches.

Running a Saravana Bhavan outlet in Kanchipuram was like sitting on a gold mine. It was temple season all year round with the constant flow of pilgrims, the school holiday season two or three times a year, and the wedding season in the summer, when people came to buy silk saris directly from weavers or weavers' cooperatives. With Kanchipuram's steady influx of visitors through the year, the three Saravana Bhavan outlets with their clean and shining interiors and tempting thalis were always full, even attracting North Indian tourists tired after days on the temple trail and craving roti–sabzi. The astute Rajagopal had noted this and had already begun to cater to that craving with a menu that was far more expansive and 'multi-cuisine' than the idli–vadai–pongal Saravana Bhavan had become famous for.

Rajagopal ensconced himself comfortably in Kanchipuram during the two-month period the court had ordered him to stay there, taking over part of a house that his company had provided to two managers in the Kanchipuram outlets. It was a compact double-storeyed house, like a toy model of the grand house he had built himself in his village in 1994. The house is located on Brindavan Street, a narrow lane behind the famous Varadaraja Perumal temple. It stood out from the other houses on a street lined with traditional *theru veedu* – houses with their front doors opening directly on to the street, some of them so deep that their back doors opened out into the next parallel street. For neighbours, an AC fixed in the window of a room upstairs was the only indication of a 'VIP' presence in that house. From here Rajagopal managed his empire until, at the end of the court-stipulated two months, he returned to his own home and headquarters in Chennai.

~

Rajagopal's empire was then in expansion mode. According to Mahadevan of Hot Breads, it was he who had approached Rajagopal back in 1999 with a proposal for a joint venture in Dubai, where he had opened a Hot Breads outlet but could not find a decent South Indian eatery for his own comfort-food craving. Rajagopal was 'totally discouraging', Mahadevan recalled. 'Do you want to close down my business entirely?' Rajagopal had asked him, because in his mind opening an idli–vadai place abroad was the best way to lose a restaurant empire at home – it had happened to others. But Mahadevan persuaded him to give it a shot, and Saravana Bhavan's first foreign venture was inaugurated in December 1999. The response, mainly from Indian expatriates in the UAE, was overwhelming. Rajagopal's son Shiva Kumaar, fresh out of a catering and hotel management course in Switzerland, took charge of the Dubai operation.

In 2002, the year Rajagopal was formally charged with murder, Saravana Bhavan opened its doors to customers in Singapore in South East Asia, and in Sunnyvale, California, in the United States. There was no looking back after that. Over the following years, the restaurant's international footprint would grow bigger and bigger. Saravana Bhavan went wherever a reasonable number of professional Indians was prepared to brave snow, sleet, ice and wind chill to indulge their craving for crisp sambar–vadai and ghee roast golden masala dosa with the potato filling just right. In the process, Saravana Bhavan had done what no other South Indian restaurant abroad had managed – it had succeeded in telling the outside world that there is more to Indian cuisine than the ubiquitous Mughlai/North Indian chicken tikka, paneer masala and kaali dal. Saravana Bhavan's expanding international presence would continue in the years ahead. In the United States, after opening in California (where the Saravana Bhavan won a rave review in the *San Francisco Chronicle* as offering 'culinary nirvana'), Rajagopal opened outlets in Texas, New York and New Jersey. In Europe, there were Saravana Bhavans in Paris, London and Frankfurt. There were others in Canada, Malaysia and Oman, and more outlets were opened in the UAE. Now, in 2003, the trial was the only cloud in his sky.

~

Rajagopal's bravado as the sessions court proceedings began may have been for outward appearances. A powerful man like Rajagopal could not be publicly seen as weak or broken by an accusation against him made by a woman of no consequence. That he was apprehensive surfaced in other ways. Family insiders said Rajagopal made several attempts to persuade Jeevajothi to withdraw as the main witness in the case. The inducements included a fully funded college education, and even a managerial position in one of his restaurants. Some family members on Thavamani's side played the role of mediators, but the efforts failed. More than a year after the charge sheet was filed, and just days before he had been summoned to make a personal appearance in the Poonamallee court, Rajagopal decided to approach Jeevajothi and her family directly at their village in Vedaranyam, where they had retreated to from Chennai, to persuade them to agree to a monetary settlement out of court. He and the other accused in the murder trial were due to appear at the sessions court at Poonamallee on 18 July. Separately, the wrongful confinement and criminal assault case against Rajagopal – this was the incident in which Prince and Jeevajothi were hijacked to a godown in Chennai's Ashok Nagar on 1 October 2001 – was coming up in a mahila court on 21 July (eventually, the two cases were clubbed and heard together).

On the night of 15 July, Rajagopal and his legal

adviser 'Elephant' Rajendran reached the little village of Thethakudi in Vedaranyam, and directly offered Jeevajothi Rs 6 lakh in exchange for her silence in the witness box. The court documents said:

> Rajendran, the lawyer who was with [Rajagopal] also asked her to give evidence in the murder case in favour of the defence. When she refused for the same and shouted at these people, her brother Ramkumar and other relatives came to the main hall and intervened. Then, Rajagopal asked his henchmen to attack the complainant and her brother. One of the accused took a knife and attacked Ramkumar, the brother of the complainant, and caused injury on right hand. In the meantime, the villagers gathered there on hearing the hue and cry of the inmates of the house. On noticing this, the accused persons swiftly got into two Toyota Qualis cars and escaped from the spot. Unfortunately, Advocate G. Rajendran was not able to get into the car and as such he was caught red-handed by the villagers.

Jeevajothi made a police complaint at 11 p.m. Then followed a night of car chases and roadblocks.

Rajagopal's car was intercepted at Thanjavur, and cash totalling Rs 6,11,950 was recovered from the Toyota Qualis. Rajagopal, lawyer Rajendran and the others with them were arrested and produced before the Vedaranyam magistrate the next morning. Only the lawyer managed to get bail. As he grasped the full nature of the accusation against his clients and the evidence, he was quick to dissociate himself from Rajagopal and the others, and said he was representing only himself.

By then, Rajendran (who would later claim he was not Rajagopal's legal adviser) had already made a statement to the police that Rajagopal had wanted to meet the Vedaranyam MLA Vedarathinam, a player in early efforts to mediate between Rajagopal and Jeevajothi, and it was only incidentally that on the way they had decided to stop at Thethakudi to speak to Jeevajothi.

Rajagopal and the others were sent to judicial remand at Thiruthuraipoondi in Nagapattinam district. Rajagopal's footwear, left outside Jeevajothi's house in his scramble to clamber into the Qualis with its high chassis and flee, formed a crucial part of the evidence that he had tried 'tampering with witness'. He was also charged with attempt to murder for the knife attack on

Jeevajothi's brother. In the rush to flee the village, the Qualis dashed against a tree outside the house and its windscreen shattered. The glass from the car was also part of the evidence.

Fifteen days later, however, on 31 July, Rajagopal managed to get bail from the Nagapattinam sessions court. The same court had rejected his bail application a week earlier.

When the case for cancellation of the bail went up to the high court, Justice M. Karpavinayagam, in his 6 October 2003 order cancelling the bail, was constrained to make a caustic remark on the rather quick turnaround in the attitude of the principal sessions judge at Nagapattinam. He wondered why, having first refused bail on the grounds that the accused came to Thethakudi village, trespassed into the complainant's house, attacked her relatives and intimidated the principal witness (Jeevajothi) to not give evidence against him, the sessions judge changed his decision seven days later and granted bail. 'I cannot but notice the change of view of the Principal Sessions Judge, Nagapattinam, within 7 days for finding out the ground to grant bail, even though the said ground was not accepted by him earlier. However, less said is better with reference to the same,' Justice Karpavinayagam concluded wryly as he cancelled Rajagopal's bail.

The cancellation of bail would lead to what was Rajagopal's longest single stretch behind bars – some six and a half months at the Poonamallee sub-jail – almost for the entire duration of the trial. He had earlier spent three months in prison after he had surrendered in November 2001. He would later tell Rollo Romig of the *New York Times* that the food in prison was so bad he'd had to spend a lakh of rupees every month to get home-cooked meals delivered to him – leaving unsaid the fact that the money was given as bribes to smuggle in the food.

~

On the day the trial opened in the Poonamallee sessions court in 2003, ACP Ramachandran recalls that raw rice mixed with turmeric powder had been sprinkled along the path used by judges, advocates, witnesses and others entering the courtroom, and also around the windowsills and door jambs. Additional Sessions Judge A.R. Selvakumar noticed this too and asked for a clarification in the open court. Rajagopal volunteered the remark that this might be the doing of the police. In response, the ACP told the judge that the police did not believe in superstitions, and that it was Rajagopal who was a strong believer in such superstitions. ACP Ramachandran says that the rice was Rajagopal's doing, on advice from a practitioner of 'black magic'. He said, 'The judge issued a general warning that whoever had done it, it should not be repeated again.'

The police case against Rajagopal hinged on circumstantial evidence, and on the legal principle of 'last seen'. The police had to prove that Prince had last been seen in the company of Rajagopal. If this was proved, the burden of proof would shift to Rajagopal to explain what had happened to Prince. And his failure to provide a credible explanation would aid the strong presumption that he was guilty.

In order to build a watertight case for 'last seen', Inspector Deivasigamani, as the lead investigator, worked as though on steroids. He beat a path to each guest house and hotel where Rajagopal and the entourage that he had dragged around Tamil Nadu – the henchmen, Prince, Jeevajothi and her family – had stayed during these trips. He collected records of their check-ins and check-outs, receipts from petrol stations, seized the various cars that were used in the crime, and collected other material evidence. The discovery of Prince's gold chain with Kasi, one of the henchmen, was a crucial piece of evidence, as was the yellow cloth with which the four henchmen – Daniel, Hussain, Karmegham and Kasi – had strangled Prince in the car, holding a pillow over his face for good measure. All the men had been drinking. They had plied Prince with drink too. The 'last seen' evidence was necessary to join the dots between what happened at the Karai Irrupu culvert to the murder committed in the vehicle and the discovery of Prince's body.

Money was no object for Rajagopal, and he had assembled a formidable team of lawyers to defend him. There was also recourse to other tactics. Prince's brother Victor, the pastor, who was present at the identification of the body, turned hostile: he had identified the body that had been exhumed in Kodaikanal as that of Prince on the spot. But in court, he said he could not tell for sure. Other witnesses also turned hostile. But, as Ramachandran and Deivasigamani recalled, they were fortunate to have on their side some who stood firm against all temptations thrown in their path. Ramachandran said he would never forget the names of Sailathnathan and the cemetery watchman Annithalan. 'This guy Annithalan was a nobody, just the guy who helped to bury the body and placed a granite stone near it as a marker. He was offered Rs 50,000 to change his testimony, to say he could not be sure that that was the body he had buried. Big money for a guy who did menial jobs. But he did not bend, not one bit.' Then there was Village Administrative Officer Nagarajan at Kanchipuram, who was present when Daniel's confession was recorded. 'He was offered a couple of lakhs to turn hostile but he refused to be persuaded,' Ramachandran said. Were it not for a few good men, he added – including the senior officers in Chennai police at that time, Joint Commissioner J.K. Tripathy and Police Commissioner Vijay Kumar who backed the investigations, the tenacious and honest investigating officers, and a sharp prosecution team – it would have been an uphill task to get convictions in the case.

But most important of them all, he said, were the two women – Jeevajothi and her mother, Thavamani. 'They could recount the incidents as if they had just taken place; they knew the car numbers and the dates to the last detail, and they stood in court and gave their testimony without fear. They are very brave ladies, very intelligent, both of them. It is rare that we get such strong women in the witness box.'

~

Judge Selvakumar, in his order delivered on 26 April 2004, also made a similar observation about Jeevajothi and Thavamani. Judge Selvakumar's prose, despite its mixed metaphors and off-the-wall similes, managed quite clearly to make the point that had it not been for Jeevajothi's deposition, there would have been no case:

[T]his court wishes to add that P.W.1 [Principal Witness 1] does appear to be a lion-hearted lady with a thousand-fold strength in withstanding anything and everything like that of a mountain in thirst and quest for a rightful cause. If ladies bravely and boldly come forward, like P.W.1 to come before the court and castigate the face of persons like A1 [Accused 1] in higher rank and range, definitely there will be welcoming change in the society in the days to come. This court will be also incomplete in its duty if it failed to bring on record that adequate remedial measures and modalities must be worked out by the authorities concerned to erase, eradicate and eliminate the fear of harm for such persons, particularly ladies who come forward to give evidence to expose and disclose the truth. The court will hope that this suggestion will not go unnoticed or unattended.

Judge Selvakumar also remarked on Rajagopal's attitude:

[It] clearly indicates his crass, crude, gross, vulgar and illegal display of 'money power' and his declaration, as spoken by P.W.1 that he has even driven away his business partners with the aid of his men equally exhibits his brutal display of 'muscle power'. Lust is like a plague which is not only contagious but also, if not controlled, will spread like a fire in a jungle. And the punishment proposed to be given by this court must be a lesson to those who get motivated by lust and craze to committing of such act.

The verdict, though, fell much short of these observations, and what the police and prosecution were aiming for – Rajagopal's conviction under Section

302 of the IPC, for murder, and a life sentence for him and all his accomplices. Instead, the court convicted him under Section 304 of the IPC, which is the lesser offence of culpable homicide not amounting to murder. It handed down to Rajagopal a prison sentence of ten years, and a fine of Rs 55 lakh. Unusually, the court directed that Rs 50 lakh of the total fine be paid as compensation to Jeevajothi. In the other case the court had clubbed with the Prince murder case – registered on the basis of Jeevajothi's 12 October 2001 complaint to the police commissioner, of her and Prince's criminal confinement in an Ashok Nagar godown – the court convicted Rajagopal and eight others and acquitted five.

The court's reasoning in pronouncing Rajagopal guilty for the lesser offence under Section 304 was decidedly at odds with its praise for Jeevajothi and her mother as exemplary witnesses for the prosecution.

In Judge Selvakumar's view, Rajagopal, in his 'craze' and 'lust' for Jeevajothi, was 'lured' and 'wooed' and 'enticed' by the words and actions of her mother, Thavamani. Her family members, including Prince and Jeevajothi, were 'mute spectators', according to the judgement. It quoted from Jeevajothi's October 2001 complaint to the police commissioner that her mother, father and brother were 'abettors, rather accomplices'.

Further, the judge observed that Jeevajothi:

> . . . even after knowing the inner mind and heart
> of [Rajagopal], from the beginning of the episode,
> for reasons best known to her, has not shown any
> resistance at all. If really she was averse and against
> it, she could have – why, she should have – nipped it
> in the bud itself . . . As such [Rajagopal] cannot be
> blamed or found fault with in entirety or wholesale
> for his 'lust' and 'craze' towards Jeevajothi.

Judge Selvakumar also commented on 'the other
side' of Rajagopal, drawing from the testimonies of both
Jeevajothi and Thavamani, and their account of one of
the times he abducted both Jeevajothi and her husband.
He referred to the incident in which Jeevajothi had been
confined in a house used as a godown for the Saravana
Bhavan chain, when Rajagopal told her that he could do
what he wanted to her 'but would not stoop so cheaply'.
This seemed to have gone down well with the judge,
who observed that with 'such evidentiary backdrop,
this court is of the opinion that A1 [Rajagopal] by
himself alone is not solely and wholly blameworthy'.

And so saying, the judge scaled down the charge of murder against Rajagopal to culpable homicide not amounting to murder. The other accused, described by Judge Selvakumar as 'arrows' to Rajagopal's 'archer', were also similarly convicted of a lesser charge. Daniel was sentenced to nine years' imprisonment and fined Rs 30,000.

For the award of compensation to Jeevajothi, the court reasoned as follows in deciding on the amount: 'After taking into consideration the present widow status and other relevant aspects, the court exclusively and entirely for meeting proper ends of justice and with a view to assuage and heal the inner wounded feelings as well as to lessen and reduce the mental agony, tension and torture...'

The police swiftly appealed the sentence in the Madras High Court. So did Rajagopal. He also got his imprisonment stayed until the disposal of his appeal in the high court. Rajagopal would not serve even a day of the ten-year sentence in prison, not counting the months he had spent in jail before and during the trial.

His younger son, Saravanan, had also joined the family business now, and both his sons were by now fully involved in the running of Saravana Bhavan.

Rajagopal still kept tight control of his growing empire, as it expanded into Saravana Bhavan's own brand of ice creams and confectionary, said to be Saravanan's ideas. By now the chain had grown to twenty-five outlets in the country and twenty-two abroad.

~

It would be five more years before the Madras High Court took up the appeals for hearing. Even at this stage Rajagopal appears to have made an attempt at 'scandalizing' the court: a rumour took hold that he would get a favourable judgement, forcing a reconstitution of the bench, apparently at the request of the originally constituted bench that this be done to prevent even a shadow of doubt as to their impartiality. The bench was reconstituted with Justice P.K. Mishra and Justice R. Banumathi. They would express puzzlement at the trial court's decision to convict Rajagopal of the lesser offence of culpable homicide not amounting to murder: '[I]t is difficult to fathom and summarise the reasons for which the trial court thought that the offence committed would be under Section 304 (1)'. Making no comment on the trial court's conclusion that Jeevajothi should have nipped Rajagopal's advances 'in the bud', or on the view that Rajagopal had a decent 'other side', the high court bench decided that while there was no specific evidence as to which of the accused actually caused the death of Prince Santhakumar by strangulation, 'the intention of the accused persons to cause homicidal death is apparent'.

In March 2009, the high court threw out Rajagopal's appeal against the lower court order. Not just that, it accepted Tamil Nadu police's appeal that Rajagopal should be convicted of murder under Section 302, and enhanced his sentence to life term imprisonment. Along with Rajagopal, Daniel, Karmegham, Hussain, Kasi and Pattu Rajan were also found guilty of murder and sentenced to life imprisonment. The high court confirmed the lower court's sentence of three years' imprisonment on the charge of abduction for Tamil Selvan, Sethu and Muruganandam. It scaled down the fine imposed on Rajagopal from Rs 55 lakh to Rs 30,000.

Rajagopal appealed the high court's verdict in the Supreme Court, and after serving a few days in jail, most of those in hospital, received a stay on imprisonment pending the Supreme Court's verdict. Now he had new ambitions to pursue. The grand temple he had started building in his village Punnaiyadi, pouring Rs 5 crore into its construction, was nearing completion. And in 2012, three years after his conviction by the Madras High Court, he revealed the next stage in his plans to expand his empire. 'We have an urge to open a star hotel shortly,' Rajagopal told the *Economic Times*. The newspaper, which described the sixty-six-year-old as the media-shy founder of the restaurant chain, said he was speaking about his business 'for the first time in years to an English publication', adding that he had 'already started scouting for land in Chennai for a 100–150-room hotel'.

~

The high court verdict was a huge setback for Rajagopal, though it was not evident immediately. The Hotel Saravana Bhavan brand remained trusted. The restaurants continued to do well. People continued to eat there as if they did not care what the owner of the business had done in his personal life. It seemed that tasty food served in a clean place was all that mattered to the thousands who trooped in daily to eat at the many Saravana Bhavan outlets across Chennai and elsewhere.

As for the employees, there seemed to be no apparent dent in their loyalty. Mahadevan, whose company partners the international Saravana outlets, described an incident at the AVM Saravana Bhavan on Radhakrishnan Salai, at a time when Rajagopal was serving his short stint in prison.

'I had gone there to have a coffee, I was sitting by myself, when I saw this scene unfold before my eyes. There was this water boy, three-foot-nothing. And there were these huge rowdy-type guys. One of them said to the water boy: "Hey you, when is your Annachi coming out of jail? The coffee is okay, but do we need to pay for it, or should we wait to pay until Annachi comes out?" The water boy's reaction was amazing. He said to those thugs, "Hey you, you came to drink coffee, right? Pay and leave, or I will smash this jug into your mouth. What gives you the right to talk about our Annachi?" Soon there were other water boys who drew up to support their colleague, and the thugs paid and left,' Mahadevan recalled. 'This is the kind of loyalty that Annachi had built among his employees. Those thugs would have made chutney out of this water boy, but he still stood up to them and defended his boss.'

The criminal charges against Rajagopal, the hearings in court and the shocker delivered by the high court brought no change in the way he dealt with his employees. For instance, for any of them going home on leave, and for anyone returning from leave, the first port of call was Annachi. Mahadevan recalls that he would usually go to meet Annachi late at night, after wrapping up work at his own restaurants. 'I would go between 9.30 and 10.20 p.m. There would be a hundred to hundred and fifty boys waiting to see him – some would be going home, some would have just returned.' He would ask each one about his family, the reason he was going on leave, press some cash into his hands. He would question those returning about happenings in their village, and in their families.

Certainly, the loyalty was a result of fear as much as respect. Even if any of his employees believed that Rajagopal had done something wrong – either in his second marriage to Krithiga, who was the wife of a cook at Saravana Bhavan, but was forced to surrender to her husband's boss while the husband accepted monetary compensation and fled for his life, or in pursuing Jeevajothi to the point where he'd had her husband killed – no one said a word. Staffers seemed bound by an omerta, and violating it would bring its own punishment. Getting the boot could affect the entire family, as sometimes an entire lot of siblings and cousins would be working in Saravana Bhavan.

There were whispers – the police investigators said they received anonymous calls thanking them for 'saving our wives and daughters' when they arrested Rajagopal – but Saravana Bhavan employees also seemed to accept that this was what powerful men did. There were women employees too at Saravana Bhavan, but if they were concerned that he preyed on women, they did not come out to say it. If at all the employees were concerned that their boss was convicted for murder, it was about what would happen to the restaurant chain, the future of their own jobs and all the perks that came with them. After all these years, the employees I spoke to were more rueful that Rajagopal had got 'mixed-up in bad company' than critical of his act of heinous crime.

11

On that sweltering July day in 2019, the white-haired man on the stretcher swaddled in a white towel and bed sheets, an oximeter clipped to his left index finger and attached to a portable measuring device, and an oxygen mask clamped over his nose, bore little resemblance to the powerful boss of the Saravana Bhavan empire as he waited in the ambulance outside the Chennai sessions court in Egmore.

Some three months earlier, on 29 March 2019, a three-member bench of the Supreme Court had dismissed the appeals by Rajagopal and his accomplices against their 2009 Madras High Court conviction on charges of murder and related offences. The Supreme Court bench of Justices N.V. Ramana, Mohan M.

Shantanagoudar and Indira Banerjee upheld the verdict as well as the life sentence. The court directed Rajagopal to surrender within 100 days.

Rajagopal's lawyers had hung their arguments on technicalities. One pillar of their case was the 'enormous delay' in the first complaint that Jeevajothi had given to the Chennai police commissioner on 12 October 2001, about her and Prince's abduction from their house on 1 October 2001; their confinement for some hours at a Saravana Bhavan godown in Ashok Nagar, where Prince was assaulted and threatened, and Jeevajothi pressured to accept Rajagopal as her husband; and their release after some hours with dire threats and a warning to fall in line.

The defence counsel argued that the FIR was registered only on 9 November 2001, more than a month after the occurrence of the alleged crime. However, the Supreme Court was clear there were good reasons to explain the inordinate delay in filing the first complaint – round-the-clock surveillance by Rajagopal's henchmen on Jeevajothi and her family members; hesitation on the part of the complainant because Rajagopal had helped her and her family financially on several occasions; and no evidence to show any motive of false implication. The delay had not made any material difference to the prosecution's case, the Supreme Court held.

The Supreme Court also rejected the defence's argument that the incident on 26 October 2001 was a continuation of the incident of 1 October, and therefore the second FIR, the investigations and prosecution flowing from it were all illegal. The Supreme Court noted that despite the commonality of motive, which was to force Jeevajothi to marry Rajagopal, the two incidents were two separate offences involving different numbers of accused and carried out with different intentions – the first was to warn off Prince, the second had the motive of physically eliminating Prince.

The bench threw out another argument of the defence, that the prosecution had over-relied on statements by Jeevajothi and her mother, Thavamani, and that there were discrepancies in their statements. But, like the trial court and the high court, the Supreme Court said the minor variations in the evidence of the daughter and mother were 'inconsequential'. The bench praised the evidence as 'consistent, cogent and reliable'. The judges said they did 'not find any artificiality in the evidence'.

The Supreme Court drew the curtain on Rajagopal's show with these words in the last paragraph of its judgement:

> In light of the aforementioned discussion and perusal of the material on record, we do not deem it a fit case for setting aside the judgements of the [trial and High] Courts . . . The conviction and sentence as granted is hereby confirmed, and the appeals are thus dismissed.

It had taken nearly eighteen years. And in all those years, Rajagopal had spent no more than slightly over ten months in jail for the murder of Prince Santhakumar, as his appeals against his conviction by the trial court proceeded to the high court and then to the Supreme Court. The wheels of justice move slowly, but surely: who has not heard that aphorism used all too often to sugar-coat the bitter reality of the delays that are so much a part of our judicial system that no one is surprised when newspapers report cases before the courts that date back thirty or forty years. There are even instances of people not living long enough to see the closure of their cases.

Jeevajothi, twenty-one years old at the time her husband, Prince Santhakumar, was murdered, was thirty-nine when the verdict finally came. She had got married again, to a classmate from her school in Vedaranyam soon after the high court ruling, and in 2019 was the mother of a ten-year-old boy. Her father had died two years earlier. Rajagopal, fifty-three years old when he told his henchmen at the Karai Irrupu culvert to drag away Prince and finish him off, was seventy-two in 2019. He had had diabetes for decades, and his condition had only become worse with the years. After he had served two months of the life sentence handed to him by the Madras High Court in 2009, mostly in hospital, the Supreme Court granted him bail and suspended the sentence until the disposal of his appeal against the conviction. Now that appeal had been dismissed. And this time the Supreme Court gave Rajagopal time until July 2019 to surrender. The law had finally put the brakes on the restaurant king's golden run.

At the end of 2009, months after the Supreme Court had allowed him to go home pending the hearing of his appeal, Rajagopal had led the kumbabhishekam of the Vana Tirupati temple at Punnaiyadi. It was a kind of thanksgiving. Now there would be no more going back to Punnaiyadi. Instead, Puzhal, the prison 23 kilometres outside Chennai, awaited him. Saravana, or Murugan, the peacock-borne child-god that Rajagopal had prayed to every day from the time he knew and could remember, turning east and bowing towards Tiruchendur every day, had not come to his rescue this time. The astrologers had not foreseen such a turn in his fortunes.

By now seriously unwell, Rajagopal's only sliver of hope lay in appealing to the Supreme Court for an extension of the deadline for his surrender on grounds of his medical condition. On 4 July, three days before the Supreme Court deadline, he got himself admitted to a private hospital in Chennai, Vijaya Hospital; 7 July came and went, with no sign of Rajagopal's surrender.

On 9 July, his lawyers approached the Supreme Court requesting that he be given more time to surrender as he was in hospital. But the court declined them. Justice N.V. Ramana dismissed the plea, saying his illness had not come up before the court during the hearing of the appeal in the case.

All avenues were now shut. There was nothing more to be done. On the day of the Supreme Court's refusal to extend the deadline, Rajagopal was loaded into an ambulance on a stretcher and taken to the sessions court located on the premises of the Madras High Court. It was a sensational spectacle, a media feast. Loyal employees had gathered at the court in solidarity with him. The courtroom was on the third floor, and his lawyers pleaded that they be allowed to make the surrender application on his behalf. They said Rajagopal was suffering from '30 per cent blindness' due to his diabetic condition and was 'paralysed' as well for the past few months.

The Press Trust of India reported that the public prosecutor insisted that Rajagopal needed to be present in the courtroom for the surrender petition to be accepted. The inspector of Velachery police station, where the complaint was filed in 2001, also opposed Rajagopal's lawyers' plea. The police inspector told the court that when a police official had visited Rajagopal recently, he had found him seated in a chair. After hearing both sides, the judge ordered that he be brought to the court, and be permitted use of the lift.

Seven of Rajagopal's personal staff heaved the stretcher out of the ambulance and hauled him up on it over the narrow staircase to the third floor, oxygen cylinder and all. He was produced on a stretcher, and after recording his statement Judge G. Thanendran sent him to judicial custody. Officials from Puzhal prison were on standby to take charge of him. It was a scene of high drama. But on account of his evident illness, and on medical advice, Rajagopal was not sent to Puzhal jail but admitted to the 'convict ward' of Stanley Medical College, a government teaching hospital in Chennai.

Then, on 16 July, the Madras High Court granted permission for him to be moved to a private hospital. A division bench of the court granted the relief on a habeas corpus petition by his son Saravanan, who told the court that his father's condition had deteriorated at Stanley. He said the doctors there had changed his father's line of treatment. Rajagopal was moved to the private Vijaya Hospital. Doctors at Stanley said he had been brought to the hospital in a 'very critical condition'. 'He had multiple problems when he came here. He was on life support, including ventilator,' the *Times of India* quoted a doctor as saying.

On 18 July, on the tenth day of his surrender, Rajagopal died of a massive heart attack in Chennai's Vijaya Hospital. He was seventy-three years old.

Ironically, Rajagopal's death sent more shock

waves through Tamil Nadu than his involvement in Prince's murder ever did. Over the years he, or rather his restaurant empire, had become a permanent part of Chennai's fixed furniture. The murder itself had receded so far in public memory that few remembered any details. No one imagined that after all these years the law would catch up with him and he might have to go to jail. To his friends and employees, the fact that finally he did not have to spend a day more behind bars even after the Supreme Court dismissed his appeal was a sign that the gods had answered his prayers and saved him from what in their eyes was a fate worse than death – serving a life sentence in prison. 'Annachi was like that. He preferred to die than live in humiliation,' said a senior manager at one of the Saravana Bhavan outlets.

Saravana Bhavan outlets remained open on the day of his death. Word spread that it was his last wish. Rajagopal had never admitted to doing anything wrong, leave alone committing a crime.

'He would spin many yarns about his childhood and his growing-up years. But when it came to questions about the murder, he would deftly change the subject. And say something like "Let's stop to eat vadais at my restaurant",' recalled Ramachandran, the ACP at

Guindy in Chennai. Ramachandran had questioned him on the way to Kodaikanal where Rajagopal, Daniel and a couple of other accused were being taken by the police to find Prince's body. 'Just once he said, "*Aval mela asai saar* [I had set my heart on Jeevajothi]," and that an astrologer told him he would attain great heights if he married her. But he never admitted to the murder. He maintained he did not know that his goons had killed Prince.'

The police officers said they were surprised by how coarse Rajagopal was despite his wealth, which they thought should have smoothened his rough edges as he scaled the heights of success, step by step. Inspector Deivasigamani, the lead inspector in charge of the investigation in 2001, recalled how Rajagopal was rarely seen without his coterie of henchmen. 'The fifteen guys who were always with him, they were all rogue fellows, all dressed in safari suits, as if they were all acting in a movie, following behind their Baasha.'

Rajagopal did know some influential people, but his social interactions with such people were limited. He never became part of Chennai's jet set. He was not seen at concerts, nor seen rubbing shoulders with film stars and politicians. A manager who was once a trusted lieutenant recounted how Rajagopal exulted in describing his visit to Mount Kailash as part of the entourage of Jayendra Saraswati, the late pontiff of the Kanchi Kamakoti Mutt: "'Here I was, a meat-eating non-Brahmin, visiting Kailash with the highest Brahmin," he would say.'

~

Jeevajothi welcomed the Supreme Court verdict as the appropriate end to the two-and-a-half-decade saga, with the regret that had it come earlier her father too could have savoured the moment. But Rajagopal's death robbed her of a sense of final closure.

'It was because of my just struggle that the Supreme Court upheld his conviction and his life sentence. As long as I live, I can never forget what he did. Though his death is saddening in some ways, I cannot accept that he died without spending a day of his life sentence in prison. Now my husband's soul will not be able to find peace. To me it will remain an unhealed wound,' she said in widely publicized remarks at the time.

A large framed photograph of her father hangs in the restaurant that Jeevajothi now runs with her mother's help on the Tiruchi–Thanjavur highway, close to the campus of an engineering college. It is no Saravana Bhavan. And unlike Saravana, her restaurant, named Ramasamy Mess after her father, serves both vegetarian and non-vegetarian thalis. Dhandapani, whom she married in 2009, had spent some time working in Singapore, like many other men who grew up in Vedaranyam. He runs an areca export business.

Jeevajothi also has a tailoring shop in Thanjavur city, which she runs with hired tailors who stitch bridal finery. This she named after her murdered first husband, Prince. Plus, she now has political ambitions.

In 2020, she joined the Bharatiya Janata Party as a functionary of its women's wing in Thanjavur and began expressing her views to the media on issues current in Tamil Nadu, such as the National Eligibility cum Entrance Test, or NEET, for admission to medical schools, which many aspirants in the state find discriminatory. She accused the DMK of 'doing politics' over NEET, and said it was a necessary exam. In September 2020, on the day BJP units all over the country celebrated Prime Minister Narendra Modi's birthday, she hit out at Suriya, a mega star of Tamil cinema, who had questioned the NEET policy in Tamil

Nadu. 'Suriya is not of the stature that one needs to talk about him on Prime Minister Modi's birthday,' she declared. In Vedaranyam, there was gossip that the party would field her against S.K. Vedarathinam, the DMK veteran and an MLA several times over, a distant relative of Jeevajothi's on her mother's side, who had helped her family back in 2001. He had moved to the BJP briefly, but returned to the DMK within a couple of years.

Rajagopal's wife Valli Ammal lives in Chennai with Saravanan, who runs the domestic operations of the restaurant empire his father built. Nobody could say what became of Krithiga, Rajagopal's second wife. As mentioned earlier, a trusted former Saravana Bhavan manager told me she took the 'honourable settlement' that Rajagopal offered her and left his home.

As for Saravana Bhavan itself, after the blow dealt to Rajagopal by the high court in 2009, bit by bit it began to lose the sheen its founder had given to what might have easily been just another idli–vadai mess. Other restaurants that were just another name in the 1990s were now jostling up, among them Sangeetha and A2B (Adyar Ananda Bhavan), with nothing spectacular to differentiate between them. Chennai's food scene itself has exploded, and a leader among the pack is now hard to spot. Despite the setback to the brand image from the time of the high court conviction, the Saravana Bhavan chain has grown. Rajagopal's sons Shiva Kumaar and Saravanan are now fully in charge. At last count, the Saravana Bhavan chain had thirty-five restaurants in India (twenty-four of them in Chennai), and seventy-seven abroad, across twenty-two countries in South East Asia, Australia, New Zealand, the Middle East, Europe and North America. Shiva Kumaar manages the international operations, and lives mostly in Dubai.

Saravana Bhavan is no longer the welfare state that it once was for its employees. Many of the perks have gone. There is no Rajagopal to call in the morning and find out which waiter has not shown up, or to drop in for a quick coffee-tasting and to check if the toilets are clean. Many of the restaurants outside Chennai now have a run-down look.

'There was only one Annachi, no one can replace him. He may have made many mistakes in his life, but he was hard-working, expected everyone else to be as hard-working, and most of all, he was generous to a fault,' is the refrain among Saravana's employees from Kanchipuram to Punnaiyadi.

Rajagopal remains something of an enigma to even those who knew him well. He seemed to be two or three persons in one: a God-fearing, temple-going man, a hard-nosed, hard-working 24x7 businessman who paid his employees well and was concerned about their welfare; and a woman-chasing predator who could kill to have his way. As one loyal staffer put it, 'He was the perfect example of how a human being should conduct himself, and the perfect example of how he should not.'

Acknowledgements

This book would not have been possible without the generous help and support of many, many people.

Nandini Mehta at Juggernaut kept me motivated throughout a cataclysmic year. I could not have wished for a better editor. Our association goes back more than thirty years. Her patience with me has always been unlimited. The book was her suggestion. But for her constant goading, it might have become a Covid-19 casualty. My thanks also to Chiki Sarkar for her encouragement and support, and to her excellent team at Juggernaut.

My grateful thanks to ACP K. Ramachandran (Retd) and ACP P. Deivasigamani (Retd), who were generous with their time and information and material. They were prepared to share everything they knew about a case they had investigated two decades ago. The details were as fresh in their minds as if it had all happened yesterday. It was a pleasure to interact with them, and be educated by them about police procedures during an investigation like this. They guided me through the complexities of the case, and helped me discover the details I would have missed on my own. They were as anxious as me that I should not get any facts wrong. Any errors in the book are my own.

I met them through the good offices of Jalad K. Tripathy, presently the Director General of Police, Tamil Nadu. He was the Joint Commissioner, Chennai, in 2001 and had supervised the investigation of the murder. I am thankful that when I approached him in February 2020 with my request for assistance he agreed with no fuss at all. He closed his eyes, thought about it for two minutes and immediately put me in touch with the two officers he knew would be able to guide me best.

Krishnan Sivaraman's help as research assistant, translator and transcriber was invaluable. His endless fund of stories from assignments in Mumbai, Dubai and Chennai, including a bold venture into the world of hyperlocal news in Kanchipuram, ensured there was no shortage of entertainment during some long road trips in search of material for the book. May he get his wish of setting up a vada pav enterprise in Chennai.

R.K. Radhakrishnan of *Frontline* magazine, who knows everyone in Chennai, connected me with all the people I needed to speak to while gathering material for the book, as did S. Ramesh of *Thuglak* and K. Venkatramanan of *The Hindu*.

M. Mahadevan, Chennai's restaurant czar, and P. Suresh of the Sangeetha chain of restaurants gave generously of their time to share their insights about P. Rajagopal and the restaurant business. I cannot thank them enough.

I am grateful to my friends Vinay Kamath, Vidya Kumaraswamy, Senthil Chengalvarayan, Matt Wennersten, Malathi Velamuri and Scott McDonald for reading through the manuscript, catching some errors and making insightful suggestions. Thanks also to my childhood friend Chitra and her husband Sankar, who gave a big thumbs up to an early draft.

Being part of a small WhatsApp group with Sudha Vemuri, Vidya, V.V.P. Sharma and Senthil, aptly named OhoAha! – a very Tamil uncle exclamation of appreciation, especially for good food – was a blessing even at a time when social media was beginning to sound like a curse. Their constant chatter about recipes and photos of their cooking experiments kept my spirits up all through 2020, but also worked as my guilty reminder about Saravana Bhavan during long spells when I just could not find the time or energy to focus on the book.

Raj Kamal Jha, chief editor of the *Indian Express*, and Unni Rajen Shanker, Editor, *The Indian Express*, have been extremely understanding as I juggled work at the newspaper with the writing of this book. Their commitment makes 24x7 look easy. Knowing that Raj writes his books after putting the paper to bed every night certainly helped as I kept awake after work to finish mine.

To my dear Appa and siblings, Shobhana and Rajendran, Aravindakshan, and Vasudha and Sanjay, a big shout out for putting up with my sudden appearances and equally sudden disappearances over the past year. Wish Amma had been around too. My nieces and nephews have been very excited by all the talk about food and murder. Hope the book lives up to their expectations.

juggernaut

THE APP
FOR INDIAN
READERS

Fresh, original books tailored for mobile and for India. Starting at ₹10.

juggernaut.in

CRAFTED
FOR MOBILE
READING

*Thought you would never read a book
on mobile? Let us prove you wrong.*

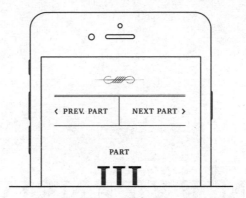

Beautiful Typography

The quality of print transferred
to your mobile. Forget ugly PDFs.

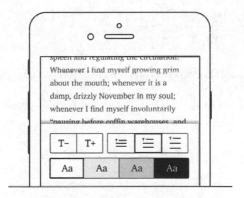

Customizable Reading

Read in the font size, spacing
and background of your liking.

AN EXTENSIVE LIBRARY

Including fresh, new, original Juggernaut books from the likes of Sunny Leone, Praveen Swami, Husain Haqqani, Umera Ahmed, Rujuta Diwekar and lots more. Plus, books from partner publishers and loads of free classics. Whichever genre you like, there's a book waiting for you.

DON'T JUST READ; INTERACT

We're changing the reading experience from passive to active.

Ask authors questions

Get all your answers from the horse's mouth.
Juggernaut authors actually reply to every
question they can.

Rate and review

Let everyone know of your favourite reads or
critique the finer points of a book – you will be
heard in a community of like-minded readers.

Gift books to friends

For a book-lover, there's no nicer gift than
a book personally picked. You can even
do it anonymously if you like.

Enjoy new book formats

Discover serials released in parts over
time, picture books including comics,
and story-bundles at discounted rates.
And coming soon, audiobooks.

4

LOWEST PRICES & ONE-TAP BUYING

Books start at ₹10 with regular discounts and free previews.

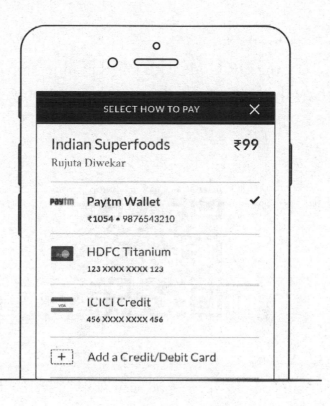

Paytm Wallet, Cards & Apple Payments

On Android, just add a Paytm Wallet once and buy any book with one tap. On iOS, pay with one tap with your iTunes-linked debit/credit card.

Click the QR Code with a QR scanner app or
type the link into the Internet browser on your
phone to download the Juggernaut app.

For our complete catalogue, visit www.juggernaut.in
To submit your book, send a synopsis and two
sample chapters to books@juggernaut.in
For all other queries, write to contact@juggernaut.in